The Small Theatre
Handbook

The Small Theatre Handbook

A Guide to Management and Production

Joann Green

THE HARVARD COMMON PRESS

The Harvard Common Press
The Common, Harvard, Massachusetts 01451

Printed in the United States of America

Library of Congress Cataloging in Publication Data

Green, Joann.
    The small theatre handbook.

    Bibliography: p.
    Includes index.
    1. Theater management. I. Title.
PN2053.G688   792'.02   81-6730
ISBN 0-916782-19-0   AACR2
ISBN 0-916782-20-4 (pbk.)

Text illustrations by Leo Abbett
Cover design by Peter Good

10 9 8 7 6 5 4 3 2

Dedicated to
> *Barbara Bregstein,*
>> *who showed me how*

and (in order of appearance)
> *Lois Marasco*
> *and*
> *Jeannie Affelder,*
>> *who showed me why*

My special thanks to: Kathleen Cushman
                        Brian McCue
                        Dina Michaels
                        Edward Miller
                        Gina Prenowitz
                        Holley Stewart

Contents

A Note about Pronouns

I intersperse *he* and *she* fairly randomly in this handbook, as that is how I find them interspersed in small theatres, and in the real world. I begin talking about *him* or *her*, but soon I switch to talking to *you*, as after a few paragraphs I assume you are considering handling the job under discussion. The only exception to this pattern is the chapter on critics. I keep them in the third person, at arm's length. The word *actor* refers to both *she* who acts and *he* who acts. I use *I* from time to time, but even when I do not, I take responsibility for the opinions in this handbook.

J.G.

Prospects brilliant; situation desperate, as usual.

—*August Strindberg*

1 Choosing to Be

THEATRE IS A BUSINESS, AND IT IS AN ART. These stand not in opposition to each other, but hand in hand; the only reason for one is the existence of the other. Theatre must survive financially, and it must communicate aesthetically. Theatre exists as much for the spectator as it does for the purveyor; it is the union of their awareness.

For the purposes of this book, a small theatre is a theatre with a yearly budget of less than $100,000—often considerably less. The small theatre will not be able to hire actors who are members of Actors' Equity Association, or stage personnel who belong to other unions without special arrangements. I imply nothing about the professionalism of the small theatre, only that its budget will not bear the salaries those union members deservedly command.

The small theatre is immediate, intimate, as all theatre should be. But a small theatre can take risks that a larger theatre cannot. Relatively small sums of money are needed to keep the small theatre going, and relatively small audiences to keep the play on. The choice of plays can be extreme, and the methods of staging them controversial. Not only is taking a chance artistically possible in a small theatre; it is the major reason to form one.

The size of its audience and its budget make the small theatre self-limiting. If it becomes too popular, it becomes a big theatre; or it moves under the aegis of another organization, such as a university. It perishes as completely with the temptations of "success" as it does with the habits of "failure." Small theatre lives on the brink of nonexistence, as utterly as any mortal among us.

I make no distinctions here among community theatre, amateur theatre, experimental theatre, and a host of other nomenclatures. All theatre is invidiously insistent. Without realizing how it has happened, you will find yourself dissatisfied with anything but excellence. This book is for those who dare not resist that urgent, lovely pain.

Theatre is work. If it makes you miserable, go from it. If it makes you happy, go to it. But do not expect to make a living in small theatre. Expect nothing. Enter in innocence and dignity, with a vulnerable spirit and open eyes.

The Structure of the Small Theatre. Theatre is a collaborative art. But it is not necessarily a communal environment. Its only essential communal experience is in the intangible shadow of a shared vision. Theatre moves in the service of our humanity, but it is not a social service, not a charitable act. It is simply, for some, an inevitable expression.

The idea of theatre I offer here is one in which each person fulfills a particular function, of equal value but not interchangeable. The respect, the pay, the need is the same for actor, stage manager, publicist. The responsibility is not, however; and the person who accepts each job accepts its particular burdens as his own. He can offer and accept help, but he is ultimately answerable to his own expertise.

The first necessity of a small theatre is the person with the will for it to be. Then, you need a partner. Theatre is lonely enough without trying it alone. And you need a fan, someone who believes in you. You are doing theatre for yourself, because you cannot *not* do it, but it helps to know that someone, somewhere, waits eagerly for what you will do. Eventually, also, you will have to find all the other people who will be listed in the chapters that follow—and a few more fans.

Meanwhile, find a lawyer to set up corporate papers and establish nonprofit status, and an accountant to set up the books. Nonprofit status will allow those who give you money to deduct it on their tax returns, and it will allow you to ask for money from government agencies. This is important, as you will need all the gifts you can garner simply to stay afloat. The lawyer and the accountant can serve as the first members of your board of trustees; or you can ask them to suggest others for those positions.

Your first official act with your partner will be to write a *statement of purpose* for the theatre. This statement will be the basis of every grant application and subscription brochure you prepare for as long as you are lucky enough to keep your theatre going. It will be helpful as you approach someone for the initial pennies you will need for the first month's rent, the first ad, the first few light bulbs with which to illumine your first play. The writing of the statement, moreover, will be the beginnings of learning how ideas can be bounced from one person to another, not losing their edges in the process but rather becoming more acute through the involvement of all. Through the years, and for different purposes, you will rewrite and edit that statement. But to write it together at the start will force you to think through a rationale for your existence, which may be inexplicable while you are in the midst of the work of the theatre. Everything in theatre is wholly personal, and wholly shared. This first exercise will test your urge and your ability to create in such a paradoxical environment.

Theatre divides itself easily into the part that works best from an office and the part that works best from the stage. Even the smallest theatre should have a space for an office and a space for a stage. Those who work in one space are not in the service of the other; they are both in the service of the search for beauty and wisdom. If they listen to each other, they may find their way to it.

Making decisions is the rub within such a structure; and there are two partially satisfactory ways in which decisions are often made in a small theatre:

1. A few persons who regard themselves as more nearly permanent than others—the artistic director, the general manager, two actors perhaps—get together until the battle is over. This leads to cries of "in group" from those who, after the decision,

can become considerably more temporary than the decision makers.

2. A board of trustees sends down battle orders. This leads to another brand of elitism, as those who do not participate in the work of the theatre have their hands in the livelihoods of those who do.

Compromise is the death of art; but the life of the theatre is in collaboration among determined and insightful people. Prepare for the inevitable battles, and let me recommend to you a structure for a small theatre within which decisions can be clearly made. It may not keep you happy, or the account books in the black, or the audience in their seats; but this blend of good intention with fervor leaves room to breathe and to change.

1. Outside the theatre, there is a *board of trustees*. These are local people who believe deeply, for whatever reasons, in the importance of theatre. They are far too busy to have much to do with your theatre from day to day or even month to month; but annually they will contribute a few dollars, and they have lots of friends who would be glad to do likewise.

2. Within the theatre, there is an *artistic director* and a *general manager*, who are absolutely equal in importance, commitment, and power. The artistic director takes responsibility for all major decisions that involve the stage; the general manager takes responsibility for all major decisions that involve the office. Together they decide overall matters involving the entire theatre —an important tour, a place of residence, new equipment of considerable cost—in consultation with whomever they independently choose.

When a decision concerns only one play, everyone working in any capacity on that play may join in the decision-making process. But the general manager or the artistic director in whose purview the decision lies must have final authority, and must take responsibility for its consequences.

Nevertheless, a group vote is sometimes the only way a decision can be made equitably, because the decision affects closely and personally each member of the group. The distinction between those matters that are of professional concern and those of personal substance is often unclear. I can offer no yardstick. But if the matter is personal, I recommend a meeting for a group decision.

Meetings should be as infrequent as possible, but as often as necessary. Each person should have the chance to speak twice, and there can be no interruptions or other conversation while someone is presenting his views. The action in question should be undertaken only if there are no "no" votes cast—that is, if everyone either votes "yes" or abstains. Democracy is almost as inappropriate in small groups as it is in art. A majority of one is not a consensus. Consensus may come when another vote is taken, after a few days have passed and tempers have cooled.

Meetings are prone to lack of focus, time-consuming, and usually accomplish little more than the scheduling of the next meeting. But a fairly regular get-together can be reassuring, and allows people who rarely see each other to acknowledge and compliment each other's efforts. When things are going well, the scheduling of meetings is often forgotten; but the moment things go awry cries of "Meeting!" will ring through the halls. Be responsive to the calls; but not at the expense of the limited time you have for your unlimited jobs.

Theatre as Therapy or Politics. Those who work in the theatre are in danger of believing that their personal lives are a paradigm for the lives of all. But the use of theatre as therapy is a dreadful and usually dreary conceit; it solves nothing except the problem of where to seat the audience, because in all likelihood there will soon be none to seat. A director's private troubles are no substitute for Weltanschauung; though it is necessary to have a vision of the world to look perceptively at one's own ill ease. The therapeutic benefits of theatre lie, instead, in doing the most rigorous, honest, daring work, and in communicating it to strangers.

Deceptions run especially rampant in political theatre. Because the world needs changing, the temptation is there to turn the stage into a pulpit, the set into a placard, the script into an issue, and the actor into a cipher. But theatre rarely solves any one problem, personal or political. To equate theatre with topicality is to distort it, to squeeze it down, to make of it less than it naturally accomplishes. Paradoxically, it is also to make less of the political or personal issue than the universal that it probably is. Of course a play can be "about" something. But if any single subject is to maintain its significance, all that it is about must bear its consequences in the full and layered world of the stage.

There is a use for instant, confrontational theatre—street theatre, agit-prop, political puppet theatre. But you don't need a theatre organization for that; you need a political organization. The scene must be followed with a leaflet, a lecture, and a letter to the editor or the senator; or with direct action. Theatre alone will not, and should not, do it.

Theatre is a powerful art. Because it captures our senses, our emotions, our minds, our dreams, we may wish to harness that power to a narrow purpose, hoping to achieve a longer pull. But theatre demands a wide scope, and it is too elegant and too complex for that scope to be denied. Yes, the world needs changing. Use anything harmless that you can to change it; I wish you luck, for the sake of your children and my own. But in order to make the best use of theatre, make the best theatre that you can.

A play can last three hours, or three hundred years, or the whole of the rest of your life. That eerie soup of awe, tension, recognition, and surprise as a live actor moves right now before a live witness is far too temporary to have any rationalizable importance. To choose to be in small theatre is to choose perpetual childhood, to do the act regardless of its consequences, to take a risk at once noble and absurd. If you are lucky, its result will be a whiff of memories, a taste of eternity, the invigoration of the will, joy, abandon, transcendence.

2 Administration and Budget

THE PRIMARY DUTIES of the administrative staff are to draw up and manage the budget, to raise funds, and to handle all public relations tasks. Because publicity is so complicated, so important, and so expensive, I have addressed it in a separate chapter. But publicity will probably be the main item in the budget, and thus the responsibilities for budget and publicity are closely related. Often the general manager will also serve as the budget director or publicity director of the small theatre; and, in any case, it is essential that she know just about everything about these two areas, in order to set realistic limits and to push towards idealistic goals.

Your theatre needs a fervent administrative staff, which may grow alarmingly as paperwork piles up. The office of the theatre can begin to feel far more confining than any stage space, and the issue of who smokes cigarettes can suddenly seem of far greater import than any fiery political question. The telephone, the typewriter, the Rolodex, the filing cabinet, the calendar are the perquisites of the administrator's reign. Provide all of them, in as adequate an office as possible. The little extras, like windows, can do wonders for cheerful concentration.

Some separation of the office from the stage provides a useful protective alienation. During rehearsals the actors really should not hear about money woes or ticket slows; likewise, the publicity director does not really want to know that on the sixth time through the scene it still does not work and that everyone is irritably certain that it never will.

The underlying question behind all administrative considerations is: Will this action cause financial ruin? The only predictable consequences of any course of action in a small theatre are negative ones. A profit can never be guaranteed, no matter how hard you try. The best administrator, therefore, is the one who can plan survival through disaster. The disaster itself is probably inevitable, and rarely can be blamed solely on administrators.

Raising money is primarily an administrative chore. But the artistic staff of the small theatre must share in this difficult task as well. They can contribute to and refine the theatre's written statement of purpose. They can help lick and stuff envelopes when it comes time to send out large mailings. They can make social calls without looking as though they are being dragged by the earlobe. And they can make plays that the administrators can genuinely claim to be worth supporting.

The general manager should keep the theatre's statement of purpose close at hand. It will be useful for all brochures that the publicity people must write; and it will help in the writing and rewriting of grant applications. The statement will also give the general manager and her staff direction at those times when they surface from the sea of details and paperwork, look about, and wonder what got them into the water to start with.

LAWYER AND ACCOUNTANT

The two members of your administrative staff who, happily, will not share your office are your lawyer and your accountant. Find one of each who is accessible and eager, and keep their telephone numbers clearly posted.

You will probably not be able to afford the usual fees for the expensive and invaluable services these professionals provide. If you are able to find a lawyer and an accountant who are both competent and patrons of the arts, remember that the difference between what you pay them and what they ordinarily charge can be viewed as an "in kind" contribution, and can be cited as a donation when you apply for matching grants. The money you have not paid them, however, is not real income. Do not figure it in your budget as money that can be spent on other needs. Its only accounting functions are to provide a matching grant for you and a possible tax deduction for the lawyer and the accountant.

The lawyer you retain will set up your corporate papers; establish your nonprofit status; translate your organization into the legalese of bylaws; and keep your guard up against violations of building, fire, electrical, and zoning codes. Some communities require an "entertainment license"; or insist on police protection for events at certain hours; or set limits on noise, seating capacity, or parking. Your lawyer can guide you through this maze of regulations, or go through it in your stead.

Despite the best of legal aid, if a community wishes strongly to enforce all its regulations regarding public performances the small theatre will not be able to survive. Aisle lights, metal-encased wiring, or special alarm systems may simply be out of the question financially, or your landlord may be unwilling to have his property altered. If your violations are not brazenly detrimental to public safety, however, and if your lawyer enjoys tilting at bureaucratic windmills for little or no fee, you will be able to keep your theatre open. The excitement the battles afford can even add interest, newsworthiness, and energy to your art.

But do not court the rage of politicians. You are in show business, not show-off business. Open on as small a scale as the publicist can bear. You will have finances for future shows, you will give the public a chance to say more of you than you do of yourselves, and you will not frighten city hall. Investigate quietly the codes of your city, and demonstrate good faith in your efforts to abide by them. Once you have a base of community support, the powers that be will be far more reluctant to shut you down on a technicality than they might be before you open your doors. Their worries about the potential nuisance you may cause with noise, crowds, or congested traffic may evaporate as you turn out to be quieter than they had expected or you had hoped.

There are, of course, also a myriad of rules for theatre unions, primarily those of Actors' Equity Association and the International Alliance of Theatre and Stage Employees. My advice to the small theatre is to avoid unions. However reasonable their requirements may be, the small theatre simply will not be able always to afford a guaranteed salary. (I have given attention to the subject of salaries on pages 16–20.)

The principal function of the accountant is to compute your taxes, and to complete and file all the forms that go along with those taxes. Even if your theatre is a nonprofit organization, you will still need to pay various federal and state taxes, primarily related to payroll and unemployment insurance. Consult the expert. The legal troubles caused by nonpayment of taxes are as serious as any, except danger to the physical safety of your company and your audience.

Besides unemployment insurance, you will need accident and health insurance for your company and audience, and fire and theft insurance for your property. Carefully review with your accountant the costs and benefits of such additional expenses. Often the size of the budget itself will determine the amount of insurance one should carry, and that amount may change yearly.

Remember: the vital item that breaks or is stolen may be worth very little in actuarial terms, but the climax of your production may turn on its appearance as the arras opens to reveal it. A systematic lockup at the close of each evening costs you no money, but its benefits are greater than any insurance premium you could afford.

The other function a good accountant will serve is to help your budget manager set up a bookkeeping system that suits your needs. It will be up to you to stick to the system, to record cash flow on a frequent and regular basis, and to take note if the balance shifts without warrant. Do not use the "petty cash" account to pay for items that cost more than a dollar; if it costs more than a dollar, it belongs under a labeled category. And expenses should be checked with the budget manager before the money is spent. Afterwards may be too late.

THE BUDGET

The budget is the system you will set up for the allocation of funds, and the reasonable estimate of how much those funds will add up to. The artistic and administrative costs for the small theatre fall into two general categories: what you must spend, and what you want to spend. Most arguments about money will be over the boundary line between these two. There is no easy answer. But it is not worth letting the theatre collapse over money, unless you have other reasons for wanting to let it collapse. In that case, money in all its political aspects is often the excuse that will let everyone off the awkward hook. "Inflation," "conservatism," and "radicalism" sound far more elegant at the end of a pointed finger than your name or mine.

A budget is of no use unless you stick to it. Be realistic when you set it up, with regard to how much you can expect to receive under minimally acceptable conditions and how much you can expect to spend under frugal conditions.

Set a budget for the entire season. Different plays will require different funding; but the variance in a small theatre is not great, except when a musical production brings additional costs for royalties and orchestra. Administrative costs should be the same for each play. Every play deserves the same amount spent on its publicity, and basic costs like rent are spread out over the course of the season.

If you find yourself a week before opening a show thinking that five hundred dollars more will save the production, be cautious. It is hardly ever just one thing that can save a show, except an actor—and the best of these cannot be bought, at least not for long. But if a little spent over budget can give a lift to a despondent company, go ahead. You may patch a psychological gap far more important to the well-being of your show than any physical lack you seem to be filling.

In general, plan to spend less money on a show than you actually have available. Leave a little extra for the director's last-minute use. It will make that final spurt towards opening special in one more way.

There is no "correct" budget for any show, or any type of show. Nor is there a "correct" budget for any theatre, except the budget that does not permit expenditure to exceed income for too long a time. The most important function of the administrative staff is to keep the theatre from going bankrupt soon.

To establish your budget, begin like this: In one column,

1. List and total all grants expected for the year.
2. Estimate the amount of income you can expect from scheduled tours, classes and workshops, and subscription sales—every source of income *except* individual ticket sales. Keep your expectations low.

In another column,

1. List your rent and estimated utilities. Estimate high.
2. Put down a sum equal to rent plus utilities, for publicity.

Now subtract the total for the second column (rent, utilities, publicity) from the total for the first column (grants, other income). The result is the approximate amount of money you have to spend on items other than absolutely basic necessities.

If your total is a negative number, you will have to depend on individual ticket sales even to keep the theatre going. If the amount is a positive number, you will need individual ticket sales if you are to afford to pay personnel and to purchase anything beyond the basic necessities. You will always want individual ticket sales, but it is relaxing to know that you can survive for a while with only the barest minimum of them.

Below is a chart listing the usual items in a small theatre's budget. Some of these will be paid for once yearly, some monthly, and some weekly. Be alert to the amount of money you need on hand at any given time. Do not fool yourself into thinking that you have underspent the budget in a month that does not include an infrequent expenditure. Even one-time expenditures must be amortized in your budget over the entire season.

It is a good idea to compute the entire budget on a weekly basis, even though you will not actually be doling out the money weekly. The weekly estimate gives some sense to the weekly point-system salary I will discuss in the next section. Figure the number of weeks in your budget according to the actual number of weeks in your season. Though there are fifty-two weeks in a year, there may be only forty on your annum. If you are paying a yearly rent, but are using the space for only forty weeks, it is a good idea for budget purposes to divide the yearly rent by forty. But pay the rent only as it actually comes due. You will gather some interest while your money is in the bank, and it can provide a cushion against a temporary setback. (To illustrate: Your rent is $5,000 yearly, but you use the theatre only September through June. In your budget, rent will appear as $500 per month, or $125 per week. In actuality, you pay out $416 each calendar month.)

Sample Budget

This sample budget gives a general indication of the items of a budget sheet for the small theatre. Note that allowance is made under each category in the initial budget for miscellaneous items. The final budget report should show as exactly as possible how the money from these allowances was spent.

The placement of subtotals will depend on the accounting system chosen by the theatre.

REVENUES:
  I. Earned Income
      Subscription:
      Groups:
      Bookings:
      Tours:
      Workshops:
      Lecture/Demonstrations:
      Single Tickets:
      Sales of Miscellaneous Items:

  II. Unearned Income
      Federal Theatre Programs:
      State Arts Programs:
      City Cultural Programs:
      Foundations:
      Corporations:
      Individuals:
      In-Kind Contributions:

EXPENSES:
  I. Administration
      Rent:
      Utilities:
      Office Supplies:
      Payroll Taxes:
      Telephone:
      Copying:
      Carfare:
      Insurance:
          Medical:

        Accident:
        Fire:
        Unemployment:
        Theft:
    Miscellaneous:
    Fees:
        Lawyer:
        Accountant:
        Insurance Agent:
        Miscellaneous:

II. Publicity
    Paid Advertising:
    Mailings:
        Subscription costs:
    Printing:
        Subscription costs:
    Photographic Supplies:
    Miscellaneous:
    Fees:
        Typesetting:
        Graphic Design:
        Photographer:
        Miscellaneous:

III. General Maintenance
    Lighting:
    Lumber and Tools:
    Hardware:
    Paint Supplies:
    Janitorial Service and Supplies:
    Snow Removal:
    Books:
    Tickets:
    Fireproofing:
    Miscellaneous:
    Fees:
        Electrician:
        Exterminator:
        Miscellaneous:

Sample Budget
(continued)

IV. Production
Set:
Lights:
Costumes:
Makeup:
Props:
Technical Equipment:
Scripts:
Opening Night Gifts:
Miscellaneous:
Fees:
    Lighting Designer:
    Costume Designer:
    Set Designer:
    Musicians:
    Royalties:
    Miscellaneous:

V. Special Projects
Transportation:
Food (on tours):
Equipment Rental:
Annual Season Opening Party:
Miscellaneous:
Fees:
    Instructor in Dialects:
    Miscellaneous:

MONEY FOR PERSONNEL: THE POINT SYSTEM

Actors, administrators, and technicians will often resent the fact that so much more must be spent on operating expenses and publicity than is available for salaries. For the small theatre, however, paying steady salaries will usually mean being constantly in debt; and no organization can continue in this way for long. I recommend dealing with this problem by using the *point system* for calculating salaries. It is a method conceived by an actor and refined by Barbara Bregstein (which is not the least reason that she is one of the women to whom this book is dedicated).

Before applying the point system, you must determine how much money is available to distribute as salaries to the theatre workers. Take up that budget on which the weekly income and expenses were estimated over the course of the theatre's year (see page 12). Add to the *income* column the income from this week's actual ticket sales. Add to the *expense* column any unexpected costs for this actual week. Subtract this week's expenses from the weekly income total. What remains can be considered the net profit for the week, and is the amount of money to be allocated for this week's salaries.

The point system turns upon the belief that each person's work is of equal value in the collaborative art of theatre, though not everyone works the same amount of time. In the running of a theatre, putting labels on envelopes is as important as directing a scene, and the person who does it must be paid accordingly. The work week in a typical small theatre consists of five or six days and four or five nights. The days are for administrative chores and rehearsals; the evenings are for performances.

For purposes of this payment scheme, a full week of day work is equal to *one point*, and a full week of evening work is equal to *one point*. If you are working on one show that is rehearsing days, and on another that is in performance evenings, your share of the profit will be *two points*.

Someone who comes in for one or two days to perform a special task can receive *one-half point*. There is really no need to niggle over quarter points. The person who gave a day to work on your show probably contributed something vital, and her expertise doubtless enabled her to complete the task in a far shorter time than it would have taken you. Occasionally, though, it is best to pay a flat fee for a particular service—the typesetting of the program, for example, or the construction of an especially challenging staircase for a set. (See "Refinements to the Point System" below.)

Total the number of points that the theatre owes for a particular week. Divide the net profit by the number of points, and you have that week's value for each point. From there, determining salaries is easy for any second-grader. For example:

Week's income $1,500.00
Week's expenses 1,000.00
Net profit 500.00

Number of persons working in the theatre this week: 10
    Five worked only days; thus, 5 times 1 point = 5 points
    Five worked days and nights; 5 times 2 points = 10 points
Total number of points for this week . . . . 15 points
Value of each point is $500.00 divided by 15, or $33.33

Five members of your company take home $33.33 this week, and five take home $66.66. It may not buy bacon, but it won't bring bitterness either.

I strongly advise against any system that attempts to base salary on need. Who is to determine need? Do not make martyrs of the people in your company, and do not make them bear guilt either. Equal pay, equal respect, equal importance: it is the working time that determines the salary, and time is, after all, equally valuable for all us mortals.

Refinements to the Point System. There will be a few cases in which the point system should be altered slightly to allow for special circumstances. In some weeks the theatre will show a net loss instead of a net profit. Naturally, you cannot ask members of the company to pay the theatre a fee for working there (although there are theatres, in Los Angeles in particular, that do precisely that!). You might want to include in your original budget expense itemization, therefore, a guaranteed carfare (say, a dollar a day) for each worker. That way, no one leaves the theatre without a weekly check, no matter what, as long as the theatre is open.

The director generally receives points for performances just as actors do, even if she does not attend every performance. She should be encouraged to come often to take notes on perform- ances, of course; but even if she does not, she has a right to share in the profits. Otherwise the director may be the only person directly involved with the play who worked on it only during the time when it was bringing in no income.

The playwright should receive royalty fees, not points, even if you are working with a new author whose work is as yet unpub- lished. He is the only one in the live theatre whose work will exist to bring in more payments long after your particular production has closed. Base your royalty payment on a comparable play by a modern playwright. (If you have commissioned a play with a clearly established predetermined fee in lieu of royalties, be sure you have included this in your yearly budget as a necessary expense.)

A resident playwright who attends rehearsals and then forms a script from the improvisational ramblings of actors can be paid by the point system during the rehearsal period just as the director and actors are. This equivalence can make him an even closer partner in your endeavors. When the play opens, however, it is best to commence paying a royalty for each performance rather than to use the point system for his finished work of art.

You will have to consider carefully those, such as the lighting designer, who work directly on a show for a brief time and are used to receiving professional fees for their services. Try to persuade them to accept your theatre's point system. It will make them more a part of your company. If one refuses, you must find another part-time professional to replace him, or else agree to his fee. Such flat fees are best allowed for in the yearly budget, and included as part of the weekly estimation of costs.

Every theatre has its volunteers, as theatre is one of the classic places to run away to. Keep the ranks of volunteers at a minimum, and their tenure short. If the work is really needed, and really continual, it deserves remuneration. Be clear in your own mind why one person is a volunteer and another one is paid. When in doubt, pay.

If an actor offers classes in your theatre on a "dark night," when there is no performance, it is true that she is doing extra work. But the theatre is also providing a space and a reputation for her efforts. The optimum course is to compute the week's tuition fees into the theatre's weekly income. The actor who is teaching the class receives a half point for her one night's work, but the value of each person's point is increased by the additional income that the class has produced.

It is perfectly reasonable to allocate one-half point for the theatre's own salary, to be put into a fund for the coming season, for example. You will want to start the next season with some money—for subscription campaigns, for advertising, for production costs—and you will probably be in rehearsal and unable to bring in money immediately. Members of the company will understand this need, if you take the time to explain it.

The income from tours that come up unexpectedly should be considered carefully under this payment system. A short tour for a modest fee can be handled like a class: everyone who goes on the tour gets an extra point for going (even if the tour lasts just one or two days), and everyone's point value is increased by the additional income. But the money from a major one-week tour that pays thousands of dollars cannot be spent on salaries all in one week. It is perfectly all right to set a maximum salary for members of your theatre, especially if you have also set a minimum salary.

A particularly grueling tour can be worth three points—for day, night, and everything in between. There may still be profit outstanding, because three points may exceed your maximum salary. Or the tour may be so lucrative that you decide to put half its income into a separate category. This could be allocated for bonus money at the end of the season, to be paid to people whose point accrual exceeded the maximum allowable salary; or to cover coming debts; or for the season to follow.

Take the time to explain the point system if you use it. One proof of its fairness is how well it stands up under scrutiny. And do not squirrel away money that company members expect to appear as salary without explaining exactly what you have done in a way that everyone can understand. If the theatre collapses, then so does everyone's job. But no one wants to work in an organization where he feels cheated or deceived.

Keep several copies of budget breakdowns handy, and be prepared to whip them out politely when asked. Every newcomer will have a "better idea" on how to allocate money; ask the greenhorn to write his suggestions down, and be sure you read them over later, or sooner.

HIRING, FIRING, AND IN BETWEEN

If you have set up your theatre as a true collective, with unanimous decision making by the group about who makes up your company, then this section will not apply to you. I commend your ideals, and I wish you luck. The collective experience is a valuable one both for those who struggle through it and as an example for those of us more comfortably settled into a chain of responsibility.

If, however, your collectivity applies only to the point system, then there will exist even in your small organization a hierarchy that determines who will make basic decisions on hiring, firing, and changes of job responsibilities. I do not recommend making such personnel choices by the rule of the majority. Some discussion can, of course, be helpful; but to ask actors to judge other actors is anathema to the ensemble, and who would feel comfortable working in an office with two out of five persons who voted against his being there?

If personnel decisions are not made unanimously as in a collective, they must be the informed, independent decisions of the artistic director for all persons whose work relates directly to the stage, and of the general manager for all whose work relates directly to the office. This chain of responsibility implies nothing about the worth of each particular job; in the collaboration of theatre such evaluation is, happily, unascertainable. It is instead a useful, simple administrative distinction, made so that the theatre might survive to do its work.

As for the artistic director and the general manager themselves, they may be answerable only to the board of trustees, or solely to their own consciences. They will have a fairly good idea of how well they are functioning if there is a steady demand for work at the theatre. If they cannot find anyone to work with them, they can consider themselves fired.

The artistic director's job is the easier one. She has the opportunity to audition actors and get some idea of their potential before hiring; and she has no one to blame for an error in judgment except herself. Also, she is usually hiring a person for only one play. The general manager, on the other hand, has only a resume and an interview with which to determine whether a particular person will do his job well. He can assure himself of the volume of cigarettes the person might consume, but other than that he is often at the mercy of whoever is willing to work for whatever unguaranteed pay the general manager is too embarrassed to estimate. And he is usually hiring someone for the entire season.

In taking on new workers, the small theatre usually substitutes trust for contracts. This makes it easy to manipulate persons in and out of particular jobs. But the general manager and the artistic director must be alert to the uses and abuses of their own power. Do not pretend to share the responsibility that actually rests with you; and do not neglect that responsibility, either.

Here are the usual ways in which personnel shift.

The person in authority wants a particular worker in a position of less responsibility—repatching the lightboard instead of handling the dimmers, delivering the ads instead of designing them. Or he wants to dismiss the worker. If you must ask someone to leave the theatre, justify your action to yourself, and be direct and brief in explaining your reasons to the worker involved. Listen to his explanations. But remember that to collaborate in theatre is not the same as to compromise. The goal must be the play, with as little human harm done as possible. To dismiss an actor two days before a show opens can seem horrendous. But an understudy who appears on stage holding a script may in fact be preferable to the stumblings of a drunken, disheveled Cleopatra who knows her lines. Similarly, shifting someone to a position of less responsibility must sometimes be done, kindly but definitely. All the members of your theatre depend on each other; and no one will want to jeopardize that reliance. Keep the work of the theatre firmly in mind, and in sturdy hands as much as you can.

Another possible shift comes up when a worker wants a position of different or greater responsibility. The actor who had some ideas that worked well in the last show now wants to direct the next one; or the assistant who has been stuffing envelopes all week wants to plan the next subscription campaign.

The general manager or artistic director will sometimes have to say no to such a request: if the person is incapable of handling the job he wants; or if the person could handle the job, but there is someone equally able doing it already. If the manager has no idea whether the person is capable, but a wrong decision could cause disaster in the finances or reputation of the theatre, the answer must also be no.

If the answer is to be yes, stay committed to the decision and to the person while he has the chance to grow into the new responsibility. But if you recognize that you have made a mistake in promoting someone, admit it, and do something about it if you can. Art does not come before persons; but the way to honor persons in the theatre is to make the best theatre in the fairest way. In human relations just as in your productions, your purpose is not perfection. The best you can do has got to be good enough.

3   Raising Money

THE NEED TO RAISE FUNDS is immediately apparent to anyone looking at the financial records of a small theatre. If that theatre expects to afford salaries from profits after expenses have been paid, one will discover that, at best, only about 50 percent of the financing can come from ticket sales—and then only if ticket sales are good. The rest must come from grants, workshops and classes, and tours.

GRANTS AND LOANS

A nonprofit corporation has two possible sources for funding: public funding, from national, state, or local governments; and private grants from corporations, charities, and individuals.

Public Sources. Notwithstanding the vagaries of presidential administrations, the National Endowment for the Arts (N.E.A.) is the primary source of government funds for the small nonprofit theatre that has sustained a reputation for quality in its art and its administration. Write to the National Endowment for the Arts, Theatre Program, Washington, D.C. 20506 for information.

In addition, each state has its own arts council, usually located in the state capital. These councils for the arts pride themselves on seeking out and encouraging the best local artists from their own states; so your theatre will have a better chance of government funding at the state level than at the national, especially in your early years. Applicaton forms for state arts councils are often amazingly similar to those for the National Endowment. Whatever surprise you feel at this will fade as you learn that much of the support money for state arts councils comes from the N.E.A. Other money comes from your state taxes or from arts lotteries like the one in Massachusetts.

One popular kind of grant is the *matching grant*, in which the donor tells you: "I will give you so many hundreds or thousands of dollars if you can prove that you have received the same number [or sometimes two or three times that number] of dollars from another charitable source." It is perfectly legal to set up the arts council grant as a match against the National Endowment grant, or vice versa—and even at the same time.

The smallest potential funding source is your own city or town. Local governments may have only a few hundred dollars to donate to any one arts organization, but do not neglect to call on them. These people are your audience as well as a source of public funding, so your connection with them is the most true and responsible of the three.

The city's money may also come from some combination of the National Endowment, the state arts council, and your taxes. It becomes clear as you climb down this bureaucratic ladder how so many dollars can be lost upon the way.

Usually money from public sources comes in only after you have proved that you have spent it. Send in your cash request forms promptly. Instructions for reimbursement will change from year to year, but the officers from the National Endowment and the state arts councils really enjoy helping you with this task. They are as happy to be able to give money away to a project they think is worthy as you are to receive it; and they are pleased to be able to justify their faith in you by your success.

Borrowing. You may have to borrow money in order to keep the season going, especially if you have received public funding and must wait for reimbursement. Despite high interest rates, it is

not completely impractical to borrow from a bank or a commercial lending institution for a month or two, until ticket sales start helping out your cash flow. Try to borrow as little as possible, and use the money to pay rent and other basic operating expenses, against the day when you will be able to pay your company some small portion of what they deserve.

Private Sources. Both nonprofit and profitmaking organizations can solicit money from private sources. Only the nonprofit organization, though, can offer the donor the advantage of a tax deduction for his charitable donation.

There is an office within most large corporations that deals exclusively with giving away some portion of the excess profit of that company. It is definitely worth your while to seek out that office. There are also a large number of philanthropic organizations, or charities, established solely for the purpose of giving away money. As you can imagine, such organizations and offices are besieged with requests. Be specific, be calm, and be persistent in yours.

Keep prominently on your bookshelf *The Foundation Directory*, which lists every registered charity in the United States, with details on their major areas of interest. On the following pages is a sample grant proposal from a small theatre to a private organization.

It is also possible to solicit money from individual donors. These solicitations must be handled with delicacy, and with an honest willingness to accept no for an answer without thinking less of the reluctant donor. Most of all, you want his presence in your audience. His pocketbook is merely an extra.

Fairly or unfairly, knowing someone does help when you apply for private funding. It can get you in the door; it can get you a more polite rejection. But knowing someone also has drawbacks. It can mean that you receive less money than you would have received if you were perceived solely on the merits of your art, rather than on the acquaintance with your neighbor. The romance of the mysterious artist, who does not go to the bathroom in the same way that normal people do, has its uses. The money that will make you the happiest will be that received for work you have already done or work that you plan to do, not

Sample Grant Proposal

The names and facts in this sample are fictitious, and the sample serves the primary function of demonstrating the general form of a cover letter and private grant proposal. Both should be written on the theatre's letterhead stationery. For more information on all aspects of grants and applications, write to the Foundation Center and the Grantsmanship Center, as listed in Section VII of the appendix to this book, under "Service Organizations."

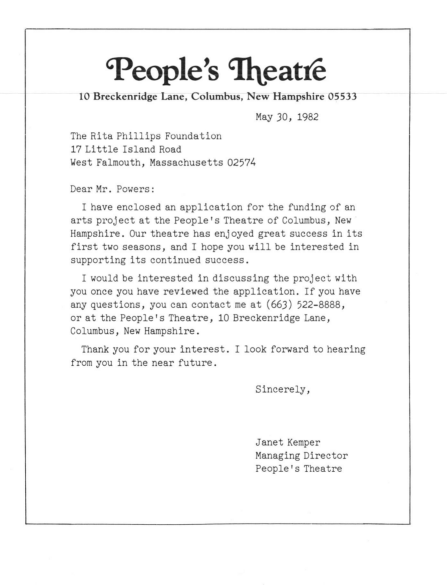

People's Theatre

10 Breckenridge Lane, Columbus, New Hampshire 05533

May 30, 1982

The Rita Phillips Foundation
17 Little Island Road
West Falmouth, Massachusetts 02574

Dear Mr. Powers:

I have enclosed an application for the funding of an arts project at the People's Theatre of Columbus, New Hampshire. Our theatre has enjoyed great success in its first two seasons, and I hope you will be interested in supporting its continued success.

I would be interested in discussing the project with you once you have reviewed the application. If you have any questions, you can contact me at (663) 522-8888, or at the People's Theatre, 10 Breckenridge Lane, Columbus, New Hampshire.

Thank you for your interest. I look forward to hearing from you in the near future.

Sincerely,

Janet Kemper
Managing Director
People's Theatre

People's Theatre

10 Breckenridge Lane, Columbus, New Hampshire 05533

PROPOSAL

REQUEST:

The People's Theatre of Columbus is requesting $10,000 from the Phillips Foundation in partial support of a projected five-part community education program. The P.T.C. Arts Education Program would extend the activities of the theatre throughout New Hampshire and northern New England, and in particular would reach those groups who are not regularly exposed to live theatrical performances.

The P.T.C. has received a grant from the James Lamont Foundation for $40,000, and has received $10,000 in private contributions. But in order to support the projected program, an additional $10,000 is necessary.

CASE FOR SUPPORT:

The projected Arts Education Program would represent an ideal vehicle for educational programs, and a unique opportunity for the communities of southern New Hampshire to experience live theatre. In addition, the program would provide opportunities for individuals interested in theatre production to gain experience through internship programs.

In its first two seasons, the P.T.C. has established itself as a serious, successful, and stimulating theatrical company. The Arts Education Program would allow the benefits of challenging theatrical productions to be disseminated to a wider audience in the New England area, in addition to providing on-the-job training for students who otherwise could not gain experience without leaving their home communities.

that which comes because your father went to school with the brother of the vice president in charge of sales.

Internal Sources. Probably the most dangerous of all sources for funding is the person who works in your theatre and has access to private wealth. My only advice is: Don't ask. Don't expect him to volunteer to give. Stay equal. If he does offer money in any questioning way ("Would it help if I gave a thousand dollars?"), say no. His decision must be completely independent, without any sharing of responsibility that might end in recriminations or regret. The only time to accept money from a fellow worker is after it has already been given.

The advantage of private funding is that you can usually obtain it before establishing your artistic or organizational reputation. Private funding can get you started. But faith will be even more important than funds, especially in the beginning. Money will be no substitute for imagination and dedication.

Hints for Writing Grant Proposals. It is true that you should gear your request towards what the organization, whether public or private, wants to support. But do not spend a lot of time raising money for something you are not really interested in doing—a workshop tour of elementary schools, for example, when in truth you need to develop a new adaptation of *Pride and Prejudice*. Money, like so much else, is a temptation, even though it is a necessity. Time and energy are at as much a premium in theatre as any dollar sought or spent.

LEFT: *The proposal should then be elucidated more precisely in sections dealing with the exact description of the proposed program (or, in the case of an ongoing project, with a report of how it has functioned in the past and how it will be expanded or revised in the future) and with the breakdown of projected expenses.*

In the case of ongoing programs, it is as important to show the need for expanded funds in light of rising costs as it is to describe expansion of programs. This places the application more firmly within the context of a successful and vital venture that owes its continued existence to contributions from individuals and private foundations.

When filling out a grant application, write by the inch. If you are given three inches of space to delineate your proposal, keep it to three inches. No committee wants to read more than is necessary, and someone who budgets his words well may, they will reason, have equal facility with his finances. Some forms will suggest attaching an extra sheet where necessary to explain your proposal further. If you do this, be sure that only supplemental material appears on the extra sheet. It should be possible to understand the complete proposal by reading only what is on the application form itself.

WORKSHOPS AND CLASSES

Many theatres raise additional money by offering workshops and classes to the paying public. There are several disadvantages to using this as a major funding source. First, workshops take time and energy away from the making of plays. More than that, if you look for long enough at people who are unable to act, you may lose your faith that acting is possible at all. Finally, your theatre may come to be perceived as a school, rather than as a place where instruction is the handmaiden of entertainment.

You may be tempted to offer workshops that purport to bear a revealing relationship to the play you are currently performing —improvisational workshops on issues for women, for example, when you are presenting *A Doll's House*. The play, however, is the thing; classes should not pretend to it.

Classes for the public do have a place, especially the brief offering of one or two workshops while in residence at a college, or the lecture-demonstration in which an actor or technician exhibits a particular skill and gives instruction on its acquisition and uses. Except in such lecture-demonstrations, workshops generally include no more than ten people per instructor, last two to three hours, and should cost each participant between five and fifteen dollars per session.

An actor in your theatre who at the moment has either less work or more desire for money may wish to conduct "acting workshops" for the public, despite my earlier warnings. The artistic director of the theatre must make a judgment in this case, about the actor's teaching ability and the extent of his acting proficiency. Your theatre will be offering his expertise to the public. Be sure that he meets your standards, for the benefit of both his prospective students and the reputation of your theatre. (For a discussion of the distribution of the income from these workshops, see "Refinements to the Point System" in chapter 2.)

A series of ten workshops can be a satisfying taste of theatre, and a pleasant social experience for its participants. Really to learn to be an actor, however, takes more than workshops. And for the theatre really to benefit financially, it must work in many areas simultaneously.

You may wish to bring an outside "expert" to your theatre to offer his own workshops or lecture-demonstrations. At first thought this may seem intriguingly income-producing, and appealing to the actors within your company who are excited about meeting and working with the renowned. But do not expect that your actors actually will learn a real skill in one lecture-demonstration, or that you will solve all financial difficulties through the magnetism of a star. The publicity costs for any single event are quite large, if you hope to make the public aware of the event. And even after considerable expense, the consequences of that publicity are unpredictable. The theatre can ask its members to pay their own fees for such workshops, although members are generally offered an in-house discount. The most useful of these workshops from a nonfinancial point of view are those in a very narrow and specific skill: for actors, Tai Chi (an oriental, unarmed martial art) or stage combat (an occidental, armed martial craft); for administrators, computer typesetting; for technicians, cleaning and rewiring of lighting instruments, for example. But even a clearly defined single skill requires practice. It cannot be mastered in one or two sessions, even under the guidance of an expert.

TOURING

The time you spend on a tour can be the most financially rewarding of your entire season. Touring merits special consideration; I discuss it in some detail in chapter 13.

TICKET SALES

The final major source of funds is the sale of the tickets themselves. However improbable you may think it is that you will receive money from public or private agencies, the sale of a ticket is even less reliable. Don't count on selling tickets. Do your best at publicity, and keep your fingers crossed.

The price of a ticket should not be so small that the audience feels that it—and thus the experience of the theatre itself—is inconsequential. Nor should it be so high that the audience fears that nothing could possibly be worth this much money. You may be tempted not to set a price at all, but to ask for "donations at the door." Resist. Accept responsibility for setting, if not a value on the two hours you ask someone to spend with you, then at least a monetary metaphor for it. Three dollars, four dollars, five dollars, six dollars are nice round numbers. Pick one. Don't be cute by charging $4.98.

Once you set your ticket price, try to avoid changing it during the course of your run. Ticket prices in the small theatre are generally the same for any seat in the house, but may differ for different days of the week—Saturday being most expensive, and a weeknight or a matinee least expensive. It does make everyone, both inside and outside the theatre, feel better to have one night that is clearly less expensive than the others. This avoids the necessity of making unpleasant social distinctions, offering discounts to "students" or "seniors" or "singles."

By all means offer discounts to groups, usually of ten or more; insist that these be arranged in advance, not at the box office on the night of the performance. For a discussion of discounts on tickets, see pages 103–104.

To raise ticket prices in the middle of the run implies either greed or failure on the part of the theatre. Is either of these what you really want to imply? To drop ticket prices in the middle of a run implies the lack of an audience. The lowering of prices is a dangerous course, an act of desperation. It will not guarantee larger audiences, but it may make people in the play feel better that they have tried everything to bring people in. I do not recommend it. If you believed your ticket prices were fair when you opened the run, there is rarely a reason to alter that belief. It may not be the ticket prices you have lost faith in, but the play itself.

4 Space

IF ANY PHYSICAL ELEMENT can be considered a necessity for the small theatre, that element is a space. Even a company that does nothing but tours needs an office and rehearsal room. The resident theatre needs a home, at least for the seasons. Actors feel more comfortable taking risks in a space with which they are familiar; directors and designers can exploit more fully a space whose corners they can foresee; and administrators can spend time managing and marketing the theatre, instead of continually seeking new space and negotiating leases.

A theatre also needs a home space, of course, for the benefit of the audience that will attend it. A theatre, therefore, should be located where it can easily be found, and easily be reached. In a city, this means convenient access by public transportation, as well as some provision for parking nearby. Look for an area in your community where people already like to congregate, perhaps an area with restaurants or shops that are open in the evening. If the location is recognizable, or can be made to seem so, you will not have the burden of introducing the location along with the nature of the theatre to your prospective audiences. A resident location offers to the audience a sense that your theatre has a real identity, and that it is an integral part of the community. Theatre itself is so ephemeral. The building, the address, the telephone number can provide at least the illusion of permanence to the curious public and the worried company. It is almost impossible to presell a show, and absolutely impossible to presell a subscription, unless you can tell the buyer where the show will be performed.

Usually you do not know who your audience is; so make your accessibility as broad as possible. Few people are habitual theatregoers. To target an audience by identifying your theatre from the start with a particular group or social class ("conveniently located right next door to the Ritz," for example) sets up limitations you can do without.

Of course, every local business is looking for the same kind of prime location that you are. And with such demand, prices are going to be high. Except in the rare case of a patron's benevolent bequest, the small theatre will not be able to buy its own space. This lack of ownership of your space is no real problem. It is all too easy to become overwrought with the responsibilities of mortgages, leaking roofs, and faulty plumbing instead of paying attention to the real work of theatre, which is theatre.

RENTING SPACE

The small theatre will most often find itself to be a tenant, complaining about the landlord just as tenants for centuries have done. You will need to use creativity in finding the right landlord for your purposes, however, and not only because commercial rents soar while the incomes of small theatres follow a less predictable course. Ingenuity is also necessary in the search for space because as much as people may love the theatre, they may not want to house one within their own walls.

Investigate the possibilities of renting space in churches, Y's or other community organizations, and schools—all nonprofit institutions that derive both definition and good feelings from the belief that they perform a service to the community at large. The theatre worker, too, believes that his is a service to the community. On happy occasions these two minds can meet for long enough to sign a rental agreement.

Being located in a church or any other social organization can be a drawback, of course. The small theatre in this situation must be rigorous in maintaining its own separate identity. There will be times when the statement your play makes will be antithetical to the landlord's basic creed. And even when the statements of the theatre and the landlord are in harmony, the voice of the theatre must be distinct and identifiable. You do not want censorship, and you should not seek mere approval—from your landlord, and by extension from the community. There are a thousand reasons for an undecided audience to avoid going to the theatre. Don't let "I've already been to church once this year" provide another.

The Rental Contract. Do not be distracted by good intentions on either side. With the advice of a lawyer you can trust, prepare a clear rental contract stipulating the solutions to as many conflicts as you or the lawyer can imagine. Such an agreement should include:

- Clear description of the space that will be for the exclusive use of the theatre.
- The proprieties of sharing mutual space (toilet facilities, parking, etc.).
- The times at which full use of the space is permitted.
- Permission to construct or alter the space where necessary.
- Maintenance of the space.
- Responsibility for theft and damage.
- Amount of rent and utility charges to be paid.

On the following pages is an example of a typical rental contract drawn up between a church and a small theatre company.

Space Agreement

AGREEMENT dated July 1, 1982 between Old Baptist Church (OBC) and the Woodmere Theatre Company (the Company).

1. *Term.* This agreement covers the period from July 1, 1982 to June 30, 1983.

2. *Premises.* The Company will have the use of the following spaces (referred to as the premises), located in the building owned by OBC at 875 Center Street, Lakeside, New York:

    a. Theatre space, located at the rear of the sanctuary, for dramatic performances, rehearsals, and workshops. Performances will be scheduled for Thursday, Friday, and Saturday evenings. On performance nights OBC will respect the Company's need for protection from sound interference. Doors will be locked between the parish hall and the sanctuary on those nights and sound amplification will not be permitted in the parish hall. OBC is not normally expected to schedule use of the sanctuary on those nights but it is agreed that with three weeks notice OBC may pre-empt use of the sanctuary for a total of two nights during the term of this agreement. Every effort will be made to avoid pre-empting the Company, by negotiating compromise measures acceptable to OBC. Use of the space for rehearsals will be assured for a minimum of 6 hours a day, 4 days a week, without interference.

    Use of the theatre space on Monday, Tuesday, and Wednesday evenings for such purposes as workshops will be limited to the extent needed to avoid interfering with OBC scheduled use of the sanctuary on those nights. Other building use may be scheduled and there may be noise interference. The Company will not use the theatre space on Sundays.

    It is recognized that the OBC organist will require use of the organ for practice 15 hours a week, and coordinating these two activities will be done in good faith via designated representatives of the Company and the church administrator.

    It is recognized that OBC will observe the following holidays through the year: Ash Wednesday, Maundy Thursday, Good Friday, Thanksgiving, Christmas Eve, and New Year's Eve; therefore, priority will be given to OBC usage of the sanctuary on those occasions. Again, coordinating these activities will be done in good faith via designated representatives of the Company and the church administrator.

Space Agreement (continued)

3. *Use of space by OBC.* With permission of the Company, OBC may, from time to time, use the theatre.

4. *Use of equipment.* The Company will be permitted occasional use of ladders that are the property of the church.

5. *Contribution.* The Company will contribute $6,000, which covers rental of premises as detailed above. Heat is included in this amount for performances and rehearsals. Heat for workshops on Monday and Tuesday evenings will be paid for by the Company at the rate of $2.00 per evening.

   Electricity is not included in the rental figure.

6. *Responsibilities of the Company.* The Woodmere Theatre Company will be responsible for set up, maintenance, and cleaning of the areas used. In particular, the users will clean up the premises, store all equipment, and clean the rest rooms after all performances. The Company will respect the property of OBC at all times and will observe all applicable fire and health laws and regulations in the use of the premises. The Company will use its best efforts to maintain proper security of the premises through locking doors, extinguishing lights, providing keys only to authorized persons, and taking other reasonable precautions. Keys to the building shall be restricted to permanent staff and one or two named officers of the organization. A list of keyholders will be maintained by the church administrator. No duplicate keys shall be made except on OBC approval. The Company will not assign, sub-lease, or sublicense the premises or any portion of them without the prior approval of OBC. At the beginning of each production run, the Company will give rehearsal and per-formance schedules to the church administrator. In the event that the theatre space will be occupied after 11 p.m., the Company will notify OBC and will be responsible for locking up the entire building (as outlined in the Lock Up Procedures). The Company will maintain and clean the theatre lobby and the stairs leading down from the lobby to the main basement corridor.

7. *Parking spaces.* The agreement does not provide for parking space in the church lot. Parking stickers are available from the church office at a nominal fee on a space-available basis.

8. *Indemnities and releases.* The Company agrees to indemnify OBC against any loss or expenses incurred through use of the

Space Agreement (continued)

premises by it or its assigns, other than reasonable wear and tear, and releases OBC from any liability arising from loss or damage to the premises or personal property of the Company caused by persons other than OBC or persons authorized by OBC to use the premises. OBC agrees to indemnify the Company against any loss or expense incurred through use of the premises and releases the Company from any liability arising from damage to the premises or personal property of OBC caused by persons other than the Company or its assigns.

9. *Statement of intention.* The Company will endeavor to be a good neighbor to all persons using the church building and will work toward a sense of community with other regular users of the building. The Company should be prepared to work constructively toward support of other groups' activities and resolution of differences between building users.

10. *Notices.* The Woodmere Theatre Company works collectively in all matters of policy. It is a nonprofit corporation, which is presided over by a board of trustees, the president of which is James Bundy. A list of members of the Company will be provided to OBC. Notices and other communications to the Company should be given to James Bundy at the premises. Notices and other communications to OBC should be given to the church administrator at the church building.

11. *Termination of agreement.* In the event that the Company wishes to leave the premises before expiration of this agreement, it will be responsible for two months' contribution. If OBC wishes to recover use of the premises for failure to comply with the agreement, or for other reasons, a minimum of two months' notice will be given, except in extenuating circumstances.

Accepted by the Company: Accepted by the OBC:

_____   _____
James Bundy

SETTING UP THE INTERIOR SPACE

Once you have agreed on your building, and have your office, a place to dress and hang costumes, a small table with a strongbox on it from which to sell tickets, and a little spot outside to hang your sign, you can begin to think about how to design the theatre space itself.

Each new play can evoke the idea of a different stage. Do not be alarmed if the room or auditorium you are renting has no defined stage area. Congratulate yourself. You are in possession of a "flexible space." If without being unnecessarily clever you can accommodate the space to the play, rather than being forced to think the other way around, you may have found easy entry into the world you have chosen to discover.

Some Terminology of the Stage. There are five basic types of stages, as shown in the illustrations on the following pages:

1. *The proscenium stage.* The audience is over here, and the stage is up there. A clear separation.
2. *The "thrust," or three-quarter, stage.* The audience is here, and so is the stage—except for the back of the stage, which is up there.
3. *The "sandwich" stage.* The audience is here, and also over there. The stage is in between.
4. *The arena, or in-the-round, stage.* The audience is here, and the stage is right in the middle of here.
5. *The mobile stage.* The audience moves here and there in the room as the stage area changes. Or the audience moves from room to room, or even outdoors, as the stage action moves.

Stages were once tilted, or "raked," so that the back of the stage was higher than its front, making it easier for the audience in a proscenium or a thrust theatre to get the whole picture. Hence, the back of the stage is called *upstage* and the front of the stage is called *downstage*. "Upstaging" an actor means forcing him to turn his back to the audience in order to face the actor who is standing upstage.

Stage right and *stage left* refer to the actor's point of view as he faces the audience in a proscenium or a thrust theatre. Note that this is the opposite of the audience's point of view, which undoubtedly has something to do both with the recent return to less precisely delineated stage areas and with their politicization.

PROSCENIUM

MOBILE

THRUST

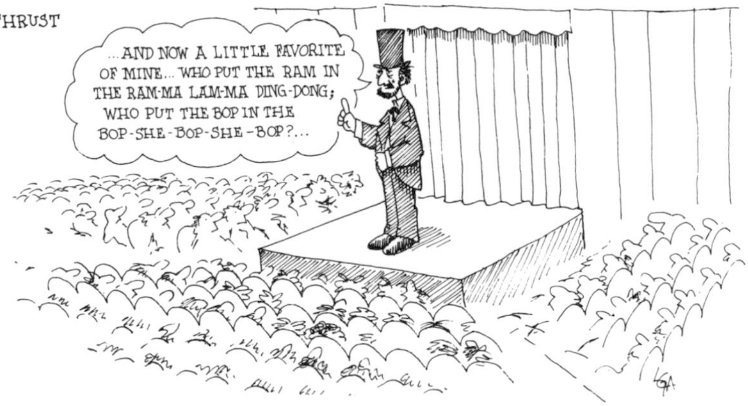

SANDWICH

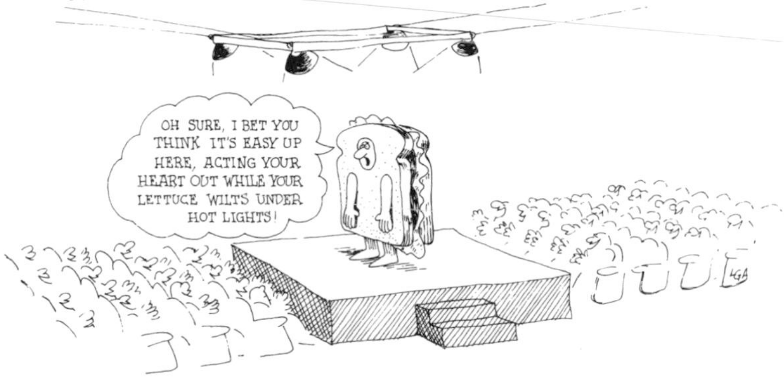

ARENA

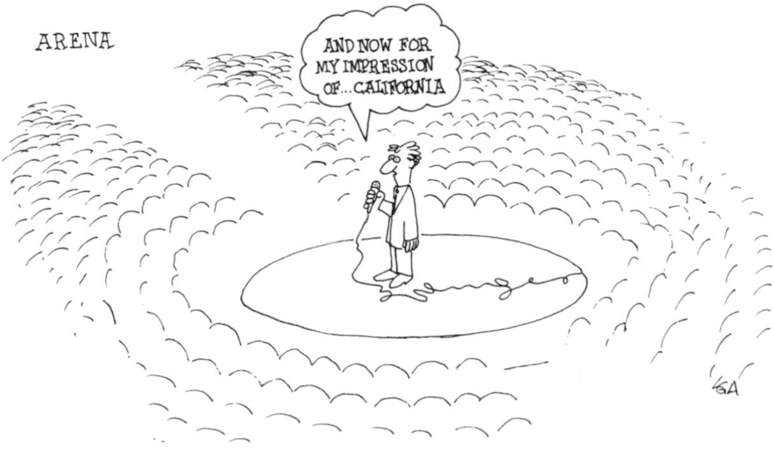

The *curtain* refers not only to the velour that rises and falls to signal the open and close of the scenes, but also to the times of the beginning and end of the play. The *house* is the space where the audience sits, and also the audience itself.

Building a Stage Area. Most stages are about thirty feet wide by twenty feet deep. Since the standard size of a piece of plywood is four feet by eight feet, it will make your life easier to plan your stage area as some multiple of these dimensions, should you choose to build a platform stage.

A stage should be high enough so that the audience in the back can see between the heads of those in front all the way to the actors' feet, without being so high as to give those in front stiff necks from looking up. The raised stage must also be far enough away from those in the front row so that they can see the upstage area fairly well. If the stage is on the floor and the audience is in raised seating, leave enough space between the front row of the audience and the downstage edge of the playing area so that those in back will be able to see the entire stage area.

Clearly, the stage can be some combination of elevations and depressions—physically as well as emotionally. See chapter 5 for guidance on constructing smaller platforms to use in this way.

Seating and Safety. If your audience will be seated on chairs, make sure that the chairs in each row are attached to each other, either by metal bands or by a bar across the backs. (Some folding chairs come with clips; improvise clips for those that do not.) No one seat should be more than seven seats from an aisle. If the chairs are on platforms because the rear of the house is raked, or slanted, be sure there is a barrier across the back of each platform so that the chairs do not slip off and cause harm to the occupants and possible lawsuits for the theatre.

Using wooden bleachers for seating your audience has the advantage of permitting you to squeeze an extra person into a row if there is a big house, and allows the small house to spread out, thus appearing larger than life. If the bleachers are uncushioned, try giving each member of the audience a piece of foam padding along with his ticket stub, to ease the strain on his coccyx. Such cushions are especially useful on tour, when you cannot guarantee comfortable seating for an audience, and when the touring company will often have to endure long rides in uncomfortable vans. Cushions also provide gemutlichkeit for each member of the audience as he makes a small and temporary place for himself in this strange world.

Keep outside walkways free of ice in winter. Mark all exits clearly. There must be at least two exits in different directions, with unlocked doors that open out. As with the electrical code, each city has a building code that specifies fire safety requirements. Though it seems nearly impossible to comply with all of these rules, you are responsible not only for the aesthetic well-being of those who see your plays but for their physical safety as well.

Access for the people confined to wheelchairs can be easily created by the addition of a ramp over a few steps and the removal of a chair in the house. Rest rooms present a problem of more extensive, and expensive, renovation. Try to convince your landlord that one rest room should be redesigned for those with limited mobility. The rest room will be useful for the handicapped patrons of the entire building, not only the theatregoers. And the theatre's share in the cost of the raised toilet, support bar, long push-type faucet handles, and widened access will be minimal. Do what you can to make your theatre accessible to the handicapped. You won't always be able to make your plays accessible to the general public.

Choice of Stage. The earliest stage was probably the arena, where the actor/shaman performed his ritual transformations surrounded by a congregation of devoted tribesmen. Our recent tradition has increased the separation between the audience, far less a tribe now, and the actors, whose rituals have become distanced through technology and cynicism. As electric lights and microphones allowed us to see and hear a stage a hundred feet away from us, the immediate bond between theatre and theology gradually weakened. Now there are only rare occasions of ecstasy when we can make that leap. How this happens can be partially determined by the placement and configuration of your stage.

Each time you put a play onto a different kind of stage, you change something about the nature and the effect of that play. It is not that one stage is better or worse than another; it is that it is different. The summer straw-hat circuit puts *Finian's Rainbow* and *Guys and Dolls*—both musicals that achieved fame across the footlights of Broadway proscenium stages—in the middle of a tent on an arena stage. The music sings in both spaces, but the audience's experience of it changes, and so does the actor's sense of that play by being surrounded by, embraced by, inescapable from the audience. There are all kinds of fun in theatre, and almost all of them are worth investigating.

Remember that the basic difference between a proscenium stage and every other kind of stage is that in a proscenium stage the audience sees the faces of the actors and the backs of the heads of the rest of the audience. With all other types of stages, the audience has the privilege and the problem of witnessing the responses of many of the other members of the audience to what is happening onstage. Laughter is contagious and so are tears. Both can run rampant; and the configuration of your audience can speed their running. But if the audience finds itself more interested in each other than in the action of the play, don't look only to your seating arrangements for the answer. Look also to the production.

There is no inherent disadvantage to the kind of stage that results in the audience having to look at the backs of the actors from time to time. There is usually more than one actor onstage; and even if there is only one actor, he will move about. The director blocks the actors so they can be seen in their sculptured forms—backs, fronts, shoulders, legs—as vividly as possible while fulfilling the purposes of character.

Choose your stage to fit your concept of the play, and then struggle with the stage's problems and potentials until it works for you. During rehearsals, sit in different areas of the house. Give each member of the audience a fair chance fully to experience this production. The nape of the neck can be as erogenous a zone as any decolletage.

I do not believe that there is any kind of play that absolutely demands a particular space. I do believe that every play can be re-seen in new, potent perspective by shocking the audience with a new stage space. As in acting, so in staging: There are no predetermined rules. The doing of the play itself is the discovery of the rules of that singular world. Making together its own canon, a company accepts the demands and the dangers of live theatre.

. . .

You don't have curtains. You don't have pipes on which to hang your lights. You don't have a raised area, for either the audience or the actors. Put your lights on "trees," metal poles on sturdy bases, and turn them on and off to indicate the rising and falling of a curtain. Put your audience on cushions on the floor, your actors on their feet on the floor in front of them. And devote yourself to the making of a play.

Decoration is distracting. Look into the eyes of the actor. That is where luxury lives.

"THIS IS A RESPECTABLE PLACE, WE DON'T CARRY ANY MUSICAL COMEDY!"

5   Choosing the Play

THE CHOICE OF PLAYS that the small theatre will produce in any season is the responsibility of the artistic director of the theatre. Actors, administrators, crew, friends, and critics may offer suggestions or influence a decision; but ultimately the artistic director chooses a play because an irresistible curiosity about it has invaded her fingertips, because she has been awakened to questions she cannot yet answer, and because she senses that the only way to uncover the answers is in the doing of that play.

She may wish to delegate that responsibility, to a guest director, for example, or to a particularly persuasive actor. But if the choice turns out to be a poor one the blame reverts to the artistic director. The credit, of course, may not.

Your choice of what plays to produce will of course directly affect the image of your theatre in the public eye. You might decide to pick plays to imprint a particular identity on the theatre itself—American premieres, for example, or musical comedies, or the classics. Or you might choose a variety of material to present in a season, with the intention of making the viewing of a production of your theatre more likely to be a surprising event for your audience.

Whichever course you take, do not choose a play because you believe that people will come to see it. You simply cannot predict what people will come to see. "If people don't want to come, there's no way to stop them," as the theatre adage says. There is a real danger, also, in trying to choose a play "for" a special audience. Choose a play for yourself, because it is important to you. Otherwise, you may be placing yourself either above your audience, and then how could the audience grasp what you say and do onstage?, or below your audience, in which case they may hardly be interested.

You are going to have to live with the play you choose for a long time. So watch out for the play to which you feel superior, whose problems you sense are easily solved. You will soon be bored with it, and with your own work on it as well.

The play that you direct will haunt you for the rest of your life, waking and sleeping. It will change you in ways you cannot predict, with every contact you make through it with your actors, your audience, your crew. You will know the play as intimately as if it were your child. Lines will be spoken, moments felt during its rehearsal with a piercing spontaneity that will never be reached again. The process of making each play will become part of you; and when it reaches the stage, you will be able to remember everything that you did to try to make something happen onstage. Yet you will never know exactly what did make it happen.

I recommend choosing a play that you enjoy. It is foolish to arrange to be miserable for a minimum of six weeks of rehearsal and six weeks of performance. Choose a play that enlarges your vision of human possibilities. Remember that a thrill can be found in the story of a wonderful old vaudevillian who still can tap-dance after seventy years, just as it can in a Shakespearian tragedy. Don't be ashamed to have fun. Laughter can disarm us as thoroughly as tears.

Because it is realized with live people on the stage, the play that you choose to produce will never be fixed, and never perfect. A play cannot be perfect, and often its imperfections are what strain so deeply at our hearts. I have watched actors perform with laryngitis night after night, and their frustration was painful to see; yet their hoarseness made their struggles as characters somehow even more deep and affecting, echoing the reluctant tragedy of their purposes. Do not choose a play because you expect perfection from it, but because there is truth possible even, and especially, in the imperfection of its humanity.

I believe in choosing a play that demands a little bit more than you think you are capable of. Theatre is bigger than life, and in every way your reach will have to exceed your grasp. The actor will not be able to reach across the apron of the stage to shake the hands of members of the audience; his spirit will have to touch them. In the same way, in searching for solutions to the seemingly impossible in a play, you will be forced to extend yourself, your vision, your understanding. You will have to acknowledge that there is more to theatre than can be listed in an inventory of the tangible, and you will become increasingly eager to discover those intangibles, to make them the instruments of your larger perception. Thus, choosing the plays you will produce and direct becomes a challenge, and a communion.

NEW PLAYS

Almost as soon as your theatre is established, unsolicited scripts will begin arriving for your consideration. Read them within a month of their arrival, and send a reply card stating your interest (or lack of interest) in the play. It is not necessary to return the script to the playwright unless he has enclosed a stamped, self-addressed envelope. The reading of these new scripts may make you eager for more. Write to the Theatre Communications Group (355 Lexington Avenue, New York, New York 10017) and you will be listed in its bulletins as a theatre considering unpublished scripts for production.

Other good sources of new plays are new play festivals, which usually consist of a week or a weekend of staged readings. Two well-known new play festivals are held at the Actors' Theatre in Louisville, Kentucky, and at the O'Neill Theatre Center, whose program continues throughout the summer in Waterford, Connecticut.

Many large regional Equity theatres—the Mark Taper Forum in Los Angeles, the Abbey Theatre in Houston, and the Arena Stage in Washington, D.C., among others—offer readings of new plays during their regular seasons. For more information about these theatres, write to the League of Resident Theatres (LORT), in care of The Guthrie Theatre, 725 Vineland Place, Minneapolis, Minnesota 55403.

There are also several magazines that publish new scripts, some of which may have had "workshop," or partially produced, performances. Look at *Theatre* (formerly *yale/theatre*), the *Drama Review* (formerly *Tulane Drama Review*), and *West Coast Plays*, among others.

Special Problems of New Plays. When you choose to produce a new play, you cannot be sure if the difficulties you encounter in rehearsal result from the way you are handling the script or from the script itself. Try not to make up your mind too quickly. It is almost too easy to change a word rather than to make the effort to express it in a meaningful way.

Of course, the right to change the words of a script belongs to the living author. The director must have that author's consent before making any deletions, additions, or alternate word choices.

The most alarming circumstance occurs when the author of a new play also directs it. Almost invariably, in such cases, some vital vision is missing: either the vision of a director or the vision of an author. As he writes, the author sees the play a certain way. It is often very difficult for him to acknowledge the essential complexities that new eyes, new ears can bring to it. Theatre is a prismatic distortion, and that distortion is accomplished because it is a world perceived from a variety of points of view, all at once: the author's, the director's, the actors', the designers'. It is a very rare author who can achieve the kind of enlightened schizophrenia which this kaleidoscopic vision necessitates.

PREVIOUSLY PRODUCED PLAYS

The more a director has read and can recall, not only among plays but in all literature, the wider her choice when she comes to deciding on staging a work. A good director benefits from an interest in as many authors, and subjects, as there are.

Make good use of your library; you probably won't be able to afford to buy books anyway, if you are serious about small theatre. And every time you are in New York City, plan to spend several hours browsing at the Drama Bookshop (52nd Street and 7th Avenue). Wherever you are, talk to the people that you respect, in theatre and out, about topics and particular plays they would like to see on the stage. Spend time browsing at flea markets and used books stores. For a pittance you may find precisely the forgotten playwright whose yellowed scenes will make you see your own world anew.

Send for the catalogues of publishers who specialize in plays —Samuel French and Baker's Play Company in the United States, Faber and Faber in England (see the appendix to this book for their addresses). They will give a short description of each play, and list details of its length, the number of characters, the number of stage settings required, and the like.

If you can read languages other than English, your options multiply. Check foreign journals, which sometimes print scripts. For scripts that are already in English, look at *Plays and Players*, a British theatrical periodical of uncommon quality.

Even if English is your only language, translations are available for a wealth of foreign literature. A translator adds his own art to the original, however, so be as circumspect in your choice of a translator as you were in the choice of the play.

It can happen that you see a play that some other theatre has produced, and want to direct it yourself. You are more likely to do the play justice if you want to do it because you were unhappy with the production that you saw. If you were happy with the production, you may want to imitate it. Imitation is not conducive to the creative act. Choose a play because you have something to bring to it, as well as because it has something to bring to you.

ADAPTING NONTHEATRICAL MATERIAL

The degree of difficulty in adapting nontheatrical material (a novel, a story, a poem) lies somewhere between that of producing a scripted play and that of creating a totally original play with your company. The adaptation of literature has the advantage of allowing a company to express its unique voice without permitting the unbounded indulgence from which a completely original work can suffer.

To consider adapting literature for the stage makes available to the members of the theatre and their audience all that has been written—a terrifying, overwhelming prospect when it comes to choosing the work you will produce. Remember: the reason to do theatre is that its questions are answerable only by the presence of living actors before a living audience. When you choose that novel or that sequence of poems to make a play from it, be sure that you believe you can learn something from its production on a stage that you would not learn alone in your bed with the book on your breast.

OBTAINING RIGHTS TO A PLAY

Any published play will state on its copyright page where to write for permission to produce it. You will be required to pay a certain amount per performance as royalty for any copyrighted play that you produce. The fees will vary, from as little as $8 per performance to upwards of $25 per performance for a musical. The usual fee is about $15 for a "straight," or nonmusical, play.

If the play is running on Broadway, or if the author is expecting to have it produced on Broadway soon, it is unlikely that you will be granted the rights to produce it. Otherwise, most playwrights are eager to have their plays produced, and you will have no trouble getting permission to do the plays you have chosen.

If you plan to adapt nontheatrical material for the stage, and if the work is still under copyright, you must write to its publisher for written permission to adapt it for the stage. Plays by foreign dramatists are subject to different copyright laws, unless the play or its translation has been registered in America. Even for American plays, renewal of copyright varies from author to author, but it is safe to assume that any work published 75 or more years ago is in the public domain.

SETTING UP A SEASON

You must start to plan for the coming season in a small theatre about one year before the opening of the first play in that season. Deciding among plays takes much time; and after you have chosen them you will have to assemble the company to produce them, prepare publicity and subscription campaigns, and still allow yourself ample time to consider the organizational and philosophical implications of your choices.

The small theatre will usually have a nine-month season, September through May, or a three-month summer season;

rarely both. Oddly, the number of plays scheduled for either season can be the same, between three and six. The particular problems of the summer season are described in a later section.

When you plan your season, remember that each person sees each play one at a time. There can be no assurance that anyone who sees one of your productions will see the other plays of that season. Even subscribers may give away their tickets. Therefore, at least at the beginning of your deliberations, you should focus on the individual plays, not think of the season as a whole. Besides, in theatre, unlike on the playground, maintaining one's equilibrium is often not the goal. Comedy balanced by tragedy may leave you flat. In fact, being thrown off balance by a play that was not chosen to provide an antonym for another play in your season may give you just the odd perspective that you had always hoped to confront. Moreover, doing the right thing once does not guarantee that the same thing will work again. Do not base your choice of plays primarily on what you did, or did not do, last season, or last month.

It is impossible to determine a season that will make full use of every actor in your company in every play. You may be able to set up workshops to placate those actors who are without roles (see pages 30–31). But your responsibility in planning a season is not only to find the play; it is also to be alert to fortuitous possibilities. You must be prepared to drop a play from your season without hesitation if necessary. Another theatre may produce it exceptionally well, and nearby. Or an extraordinary actor may join your company for a brief time; you may know the ideal play for him, and now may be the only time you can do it together. Every director has several plays in a drawer that he has been hoping to do someday. But you cannot put an actor in a drawer.

Timing Considerations. Plan your season with a calendar in front of you. The usual run of a play in the small theatre season is eight to ten weeks; and generally six to eight weeks is allotted for rehearsal of each play. The exception to this pattern is the play that is completely created and scripted by the company, perhaps with a resident playwright. This process can take a full year, or more, and still have a 99 percent chance of never achieving finished production. Some of the remaining one percent of company-created plays have been remarkable and revolutionary; the Open Theatre's "The Serpent" and "Terminal" number among them. But beware of trying to squeeze a completely original work into a few squares on your desk calendar.

Of course, one play can be in rehearsal while another is in performance. But allow the play in performance at least a week to affirm itself before plunging its actors into other depths. In fact, even if the next play involves a completely different group of actors (unlikely in small theatre) but is happening on the same stage (very likely in small theatre), still wait that week. Any sooner will feel like a trespass on this new-found land.

Remember as you plan your season that money will not be coming in during the first rehearsal period. You must decide which will prove more useful in the long run: a very brief rehearsal period, or an extravagant opening play for the season. You will be lucky if you can find a challenging play that does not require your standard rehearsal period. A common solution, although not the best, is to open the season with a play from the previous season. This allows you to bring in a paying audience with a very brief rehearsal period. But it indicates either an abundant faith in the popularity of the play with the audience, or a paucity of imagination and willingness to take risks with a different play. A happier solution is to save money from the previous season to carry you through the first rehearsal period of the new one.

A typical calendar for the nonsummer season of a small theatre company producing five plays over the period of nine months might look like this:

Sample Straight Run Calendar

Performances are on Thursdays through Saturdays at 8 p.m. Play 3, which is for children, is performed daily at 2:00.

September 8:	Begin rehearsals for Play 1
October 8:	Play 1 opens
November 10:	Begin rehearsals for Play 2
November 21:	Play 1 closes
November 23:	Put-in for Play 2
November 24 to	
December 2:	Dress rehearsals and possible previews

December 3:	Play 2 opens
December 9:	Begin rehearsals for Play 3 (children's play)
December 20:	Play 3 opens
January 2:	Play 3 closes
January 11:	Rehearsals begin for Play 4
January 25:	Begin brush-up rehearsals of Play 1 for tour
January 30:	Play 2 closes
February 1–13:	Two-week tour
February 15 to March 11:	Series of afternoon and evening workshops, on Mondays and Thursdays
March 11:	Open Play 4
March 22:	Begin rehearsals for Play 5
March 29:	Rehearsals for Play 5 interrupted by brush-ups for Play 3
April 4–10:	Play 3 reopens with daily matinees
April 12:	Resume Play 5 rehearsals
May 1:	Play 4 closes
May 8:	Put-in for Play 5
May 9–12:	Dress rehearsals and possible previews
May 13:	Open Play 5
June 19:	Close Play 5

Running Plays in Repertory. Repertory theatre means that two or more plays are being presented concurrently, on different nights of the week or at different times of the day. The procedure of changing sets, changing roles, and changing advertising can be both exhausting and exhilarating; but for the really small theatre it is probably not worth attempting, unless one of the plays is a children's matinee. For an elaborate and intriguing argument for repertory rotation, see Robert Brustein's book *Making Scenes*, which is concerned with the repertory situation at Yale University in particular, and the benefits of repertory theatre in general.

A calendar for a repertory theatre company presenting five plays over a nine-month season might look something like the example on the following pages.

Summer Theatre. The small summer theatre company is not the traditional "summer stock" theatre. Summer stock now refers to theatres that present Equity companies that travel to "melody tents" in resort areas with prerehearsed "package" shows. These

Sample Repertory Calendar

Note: "A" represents Play Number 1, "B" is Play Number 2, and so forth. Rehearsal periods are not indicated except for immediately after the tours, because they are dependent on the logistics of time, space, and personnel that fluctuate from show to show.

SEPTEMBER

S	M	Tu	W	Th	F	S
	–	–	A	A	A	A A
A A	–	A	A	A	A	A A
A A	–	A	A	A	A	A A
A A	–	A	A	A	A	A A
A A	–	A	A			

OCTOBER

S	M	Tu	W	Th	F	S
				A	A	A A
A A	–	A	A	A	A	A A
A A	–	TOUR..............				
TOUR.....................						
TOUR.....................						

NOVEMBER

S	M	Tu	W	Th	F	S
TOUR.....................						
TOUR.....................						
REHEARSAL................						
REHEARSAL................						
TECH...						

DECEMBER

S	M	Tu	W	Th	F	S
		TECH..		B	B	B B
B B	–	B	B	B	B	B B
TECH........				C	C	C C
C C	–	VACATION.......				
....		B	B	B		

JANUARY

S	M	Tu	W	Th	F	S
					C	C C
B B	–	B	B	B	C	C B
B C	–	C	C	C	B	B
TECH........				D	D	D D
D D	–	C	C	D	B	B C
C B						

FEBRUARY

S	M	Tu	W	Th	F	S
	–	B	B	C	D	D B
B B	–	D	C	C	C	D
D C	–	C	D	D	D	D D
D D	–	D	D	B	B	B C
C D						

MARCH

S	M	Tu	W	Th	F	S
	-	D	D	D	D	D D
D D	-	D	D	D	D	D
D D	-	D	D	C	C	C
TOUR..................						
TOUR........						

APRIL

S	M	Tu	W	Th	F	S
TOUR....						
TOUR................						
REHEARSAL............						
REHEARSAL...........						
REHEARSAL.........						

MAY

S	M	Tu	W	Th	F	S
						TECH
TECH.........			E	E	E E	
E E	-	E	E	E	E	E E
E E	-	E	E	E	E	E E
E E	-	E	E	E	E	E E
-	-					

shows—musicals, domestic dramas with moral certainty and justifiable conclusions, light comedies—usually headline a recognizable name and feature actors auditioned in New York or Los Angeles. They play in any one of the "straw hat circuit" theatres for a week or two before moving on to the next resort. There are only a few remaining union summer theatres, such as the Williamstown Theatre Festival in Williamstown, Massachusetts, which have permanent summer companies that rehearse and perform a series of plays.

For the small nonunion theatre, the summer season should be planned using the same rules as for chillier times of year. The froth is for the sea, not for the stage. There is no reason that the plays you choose for the summer season need be different in character from your nonsummer productions; the popularity of summer Shakespeare festivals should offer sufficient proof of that.

No matter what plays you choose, you will not be able to guarantee an audience; you might as well choose a play that you really want to do.

In summer, of course, you have only one-third the time to work with, compared to the nine-month season just past. Your choice is either to cut the number of plays you produce by two-thirds, or to spend only one-third the time in rehearsal that you might in the nonsummer season.

There are advantages to both courses. For the summer season it is often exciting to make rehearsal periods as brief as possible and, therefore, productions as spontaneous as possible. Though it is not true that for every three-act play you can produce three one-act plays, it is fun to try to do two one-act plays in place of a three-act play.

Work expands to fill the time available: again, the usual number of plays produced in a summer season is about the same as for a nonsummer season, three to six; though each will run for an average of only two to four weeks. During the summer, a theatre will often run two plays in repertory: a children's play in the afternoon, for example, and in the evening a play for those who live under the illusion that they are grown up. Precisely because it is summer, it is possible to present plays at odd times of the day. Playgoers are at leisure, not at work. Various locations— the hotel porch, the beach, the park—provide a natural setting that would be unwelcoming in a less clement season. Of course, rain can cancel or move a performance. Remember, performing out of doors makes special demands on the voices of actors; and the temptations for the audience's eyes, minds, and feet to wander are as broad as the sky and the stretch of greensward.

The small summer theatre is even more temporary than the theatre of the academic season. In all theatres, however, any illusion of permanence is shattered nightly by the curtain itself. The sign at the end of the play is a metaphor for the inevitable conclusion of any theatre, large or small.

Other Considerations. As your imagination deepens, it is prudent to look realistically at the resources that are available to your small theatre. In each season, your choice of plays will be determined by other relationships than solely that of the director to the play. Do not neglect to consider:

• The number of persons you can afford to keep around: actors, stagehands, administrators.

• The number of objects you can afford to keep around them. If you desire realism on the stage, you need the space in which to mimic it and the dealer in domestic furniture willing to lend it to you. If you choose a play with many changes of scenery, you will need an army of volunteer running crew to move the sets, as it is unlikely that any small theatre will have the engineered movable stages that encumber the more spectacular productions of larger theatres.

• The skills of the persons and resources you have around. If no one can sing or dance, probably *Candide* is not your best choice, even if you've always loved Leonard Bernstein and Voltaire. Or if you want to do a period play—a Restoration comedy, perhaps, or an improvisational medieval Commedia— you will need either trained actors or the time to train them.

Each play that you choose for your season must be equally loved. The commitment to each must be equal. Obviously, the technical demands and the amount of money you must spend on each will vary. But if you equate money with commitment, small theatre is probably not the vocation for you. Make a realistic assessment of your available resources: people, space, things, money. If any one production makes inordinate demands on your budget or your crew, another production in the season must have the possibility of full realization with a minimum expenditure of money and sweat. Do not expect the more elaborate production, however, to be the one most in demand. There is very little relation between the amount of money spent on a show and the sensibility that emerges from it; and the audience will not be fooled. If a show requires special effects that your theatre really can't afford to purchase, you will either have to make do with the effects of the imagination or you will have to put the play in the drawer. There is another play. But do not despair too soon.

The limits of physical and personal resources can often be the inspiration for an imaginative restructuring of plays, both the seemingly tired and the scarily brilliant ones. It is the unlikely that is most beckoning to the theatre worker, not the impossible. London's Young Vic Theatre, the once poor cousin to the established Old Vic (now failing financially), presented William

Shakespeare's *Troilus and Cressida* on a stage bare save for a few square yards of sand. There was a world truly in those grains.

When a Play "Fails." "Suppose they gave a play and nobody came." If this happens to you with a production in whose worth you trust, as it probably does at least once to anyone in small theatre, think through the consequences of keeping the play running. Meet with everyone involved in the play—actors, technicians, administrators. In the end, of course, the director and the general manager must take responsibility for the decision. Remember: the consequences will be both artistic and financial. The sense of self can sometimes be enhanced by persisting in what one believes in doing, just as the sense of self can be diminished by too much reliance on the approval of audiences or critics.

Much more difficult is the situation when you do not yourself believe in the play you are doing. To look at a play that you directed and to have no faith in it is even harder than to look at your own work when others have no faith in it. What are your choices in this predicament?

1. You can close the play. People will be hurt by this: the actors as well as all the others who worked hard on the production. Close it if you feel you must, and take upon yourself the full responsibility for both the failure of the play and its closing.

2. You can keep the play running, and squeeze in rehearsal time to make changes. The play may improve. But be wary of making the play, and the situation, worse. Everyone may continually lose faith, energy, and will, in this show and in the one they are planning to do next.

3. You can let the play stand for the assigned run. And try to forget about its shortcomings as you work on your next production.

Whatever you decide, this sad circumstance is one of the most painful of the many painful circumstances in the running of a small theatre. My speaking of the closing of a play in the same chapter in which I speak of the choosing of a play is not without thought. Success is very rare in the world of small theatre. When success occurs, it is often only partial. It may be just because success is so rare, so haphazard and unpredictable, that we choose to establish a theatre. We give ourselves a season of chances, rather than a single chance on one play, for one month, once in one's lifetime.

6   Director

TOTUS MUNDUS AGIT HISTRIONEM may indeed be true. But as far as the director is concerned, all the stage had better be a world: organic, complex, vital; safe for the bodies of actors but stunning with danger to their, and therefore all, souls.

The essential job of the director is really to direct a particular play, with particular actors, for a particular period of time. The director seeks answers to the questions that pursue her dreams, by attending to the persons who walk around or stand still on the stage.

The director sets up boundaries, the division between the so-called real world and the stage. The real world has its commandments, but the stage discovers its own rules moment by moment. The boundaries are predetermined by the director in consultation with the script, but the rules are not. The rules are made and broken in the ecstasies of confrontation that form the pattern of the play.

The director watches.

The director allows herself to be moved by what she sees, hears.

The director welcomes surprise.

The director is alert to what appears new, to what appears eternal, and to those magical times when they are one and the same.

The most important attribute of the director is a sensitive stomach. And the most important obligation of the director is not to ignore its warnings.

The director must prepare herself to be the creator of a world, and yet not to be God. The seductive danger is apparent. Inevitably, though, the audience shatters the illusion of godhead. In the presence of an audience, the director is impotent. She cannot stop the show; she cannot apologize for it; she cannot even take the credit for it.

No matter what the director thinks of, the actor does it. If there is the luck of magic, it is the actor's doing. The bonds in theatre that are most durable, and most ineffable, are the bonds between one actor in his double identity and another actor in his. Side by side with these bonds—equally intense, equally inexplicable—are the bonds between the actor and the audience, in their willing suspension of the real world. In these moments, the director belongs to the past. The theatre is only now. The director is welcome to the blame, but let the actor take the credit.

The Artistic Director and Others. The artistic director of a small theatre—or a large one—is responsible for the aesthetic statement of the theatre in the long run. Most artistic directors of theatres are also directors of plays, and are therefore obligated to assume a generosity of spirit with regard to the different visions of others who may direct plays at the theatre. The artistic director must know when to accept those different visions, when and how to suggest alterations, and when the best path is the one that leads farthest from those visions.

As it is often impossible to be sure of the best course, the term "guest director" is frequently used when directors other than the artistic director stage plays at the theatre. This label works to absolve the artistic director of more than minimal responsibility if the play differs drastically from the usual fare at your theatre. In addition, it encourages the habit of welcoming risks in a small theatre that might otherwise strangle on its own insularity.

It is possible for a small theatre to have more than one director on its staff. If this is the case, it is essential to construct the lines of power carefully and openly. If each director is to have absolute authority in his production, with no obligation to act on the notes of others, so be it. If one director is more equal than others, in the choice of play or its realization, then be alert to the inevitable, rivalrous clash of vision. Someone will have to give; and it is not necessarily art that belongs to the victor.

Once a director has been charged with the responsibility to direct a play, let him. If the disaster is so overwhelming that the artistic director cannot sit in her own theatre without becoming nauseated or writhing in rage, then let her leave for a while, or take over the production, or take it out of the season. The artistic director cannot stay around a company of actors and chew her program, and expect that company to put forward its faithful and dedicated artistic best. If it's bad, don't make things worse. Let them be, improve them, or remove them.

RULES FOR THE DIRECTOR

1. Be familiar with the script. The director must know everything she can about the script, including the meanings of every word. Yet she cannot close her mind to its implications, nor to the manners in which those implications can be accomplished. In fact, the director will never know everything about the script. A play is not a novel, which can be understood vicariously. Those actors who live within the script will know more about it than the director ever can. Give them the freedom to play with their roles, their lines, each other.

2. Be honest with yourself. Do not deceive yourself that something in a play makes a statement when in fact it is incoherent. Do not tell yourself that something is working organically, without contrivance, when in fact it is predictable, unfounded, and silly.

3. Be tender with others. And that means everyone: actors, technicians, administrators. Because the director can do nothing, really, but talk, and because she so often knows how far from the mark things have gone, it is easy for her to assign blame. But to be demanding is not to blame. In order that each task of the theatre's group chore be done with a full heart, the director must be unrelenting but compassionate. Her sympathies will alter the form of her demands, not their nature.

From actors, the director demands an essential vulnerability. Without it the actor, the director, and the audience will not know what the truest, deepest responses are to the script and to the actions of those who live within it. The director must be unsatisfied until she can tear away the actor's defenses so that the heart of the character can be exposed. But that heart must beat in the director's hands. Hold it tenderly.

Technicians and administrators do not take curtain calls. Neither does the director, but she does often receive critical mention. The work of those who receive no public thanks is as essential to the creation of the theatre's world as the actors' is. The obligation of the director is not to forget those off the stage, and the tenderness their energy merits.

4. *Set sensible limits.* Set the limits made reasonable by the time you have for rehearsals, the space you have for the action onstage, the safety of the actors, and your own familiarity with the script. Having a purpose at the beginning of each day makes it somewhat easier to know when those limits have been exceeded. And except with regard to safety, a little excess every once in a while is not so bad. Do not expect perfection. There is always more than one rehearsal, and imperfection can be a sign of life.

5. *Make decisions when necessary.* The director is responsible, ultimately, for everything that happens on the stage. Be as honest as you can with the reasons for your decision, but make it neither too soon nor too late. Do not expect others to decide for you, and do not ask them to, whether it is for an actor to retain one gesture and discard another, or whether the light is too bright or too dim, or whether the play must open now or later or never. Embrace the consequences.

6. *Respect every hand and every thing that touches the stage, and every person on that stage.* Respect will make it mighty, like a newborn child; the delicate passion that you have brought into being in the world of the stage will take on a sudden power, win you over, change you utterly.

7   Actor

THERE ARE NO ESSENTIALS FOR ACTORS, despite the legends of well-endowed sweaters discovered in Hollywood drug stores. Yes, Robert Redford is tall, blond, handsome; but Michael Dunn is four feet five inches in height, and his chin protrudes. Mr. Dunn can move us as deeply as the most classic ideal of male forms.

Can anyone be an actor? No. There is trouble if you try to sing "Un Bel Di" without a sense of pitch. There is trouble if you attempt to dance *Swan Lake* without a sense of balance. And there is trouble if you dare to act without courage, skill, stamina, sympathy. Even if you possess all of these, there are no guarantees. Being an actor has something to do with imagination made flesh; and with the willingness—even the need—to permit others to recognize it, to be charged by it, to be undone by it. You will know if you are an actor at that moment you feel yourself to be most alive on stage, in a union with some eternal figure that exceeds sexuality. At that moment, the approval of an audience, or the lack of it, will matter less than the dropping of a leaf to the ground. A kind of ecstasy you will not recognize until later will inform your spirit, will lift your voice, will shape your presence. You will be thanked. You will thank the heavens.

TEN BASIC EXERCISES FOR ACTORS

1. *Observe the world.* I recommend long walks, rides on public transportation, browsing in department stores and on piers. It is necessary to bring the world to the stage, and you will be responsible for much of that world's being there. Let yourself be vulnerable to all that you observe. Allow people, things, events, coincidences of sensation to imprint themselves on your sensibility; and enjoy a respect for those marks.

2. *Do athletics.* Find a sport that is not necessarily competitive but that demands physical communication with another person, either as opponent or partner. It will tune your body, sharpen your sense of timing, make more comfortable your awareness that stimulus merits response. And it will keep you involved in a heightened activity. Anything from ping-pong to water polo will do, with bicycles built for two falling somewhere in the middle. Team sports are fine, but you have a responsibility to keep your body healthy, so don't go out for football; and do not depend on sports that await the appearance of twenty-one others.

Physical disability does not prevent one's doing athletics, or being an actor. The deaf can wrestle, the blind can indulge in a myriad of sound-signaled games. Actors with limited mobility should make use of whatever range of movement they do have, and maintain communication with that partner or opponent with a minimum of spoken English and as much body English as possible.

I have worked with actors with limited vision, actors with limited hearing, and actors confined to wheelchairs; and I found their potential to communicate and to affect as strong as that of the (temporarily) able-bodied. This was true neither because of the handicap nor despite it, but because they were actors. In her short story "Tempests," which is about Shakespeare's play, Isak Dinesen writes of the possible descent of a fairy into the rehearsal hall. That fairy could not play Ariel, the director says, because he has wings and he can fly.

Acting is the being there for another. Just as you do not have to be chairbound to represent Elizabeth Barrett in *The Barretts of Wimpole Street*, so you do not have to be able to walk in order to move with sturdy purpose through Henrik Ibsen's houses.

3. *Use your voice.* Memorize ten lines of William Shakespeare for one week during each month. For the other three weeks, play with them on your lips, on your tongue, and on your breath (or on your fingers, if you are deaf). Beyond the limbering this achieves, you will gain a habitual acquaintance with the master of the stage and with the most enduring and profound of its language, its people, its implications. Besides, you will never be at a loss for an audition piece or an aphorism.

4. *Use your body.* Move, in whatever way feels comfortable, in one direction. Then move the same way in the other direction. Rest for half the interval that you have moved. Sense as you move the shape your body takes, or the rhythms it falls prey to. Repeat those shapes and rhythms that feel either most comfortable or most alluring. Become gradually self-aware (as opposed to self-conscious) as you move, so that you can remember, repeat, vary, and enjoy your own body and its temporary occupation of space.

Do not try to create the same pattern day after day. But do not try, either, to be cleverly different. Do not hurt yourself physically. Do not begin by stretching to your limits. As you build up to them, your limits will begin to expand. Secret: Say those Shakespeare lines as you move the separate parts of your articulate body.

Any movement to music is useful and fun, but beware dancing and mime. They may both permit you to rely on some predetermined pattern, and thus to ignore your own bounding impulses. Of course, the actor who is skilled at singing, dance, or mime is able to perform in many types of plays, and he has at his command a range of expression for the characters he plays. Do not confuse the mode of expression with the thing expressed, however. The mime who cannot act is truly kin to the robot, and the singer who cannot communicate a character may shatter the champagne goblet, but he will never make an audience burst into tears. The dancer, moreover, runs the risk of becoming unable to take a natural step. Rule of thumb: Whatever amount of time you spend honing these skills, spend an equal amount of time going through the searching exercises.

5. *Let your body and your voice transform themselves.* You will become an object, an animal, another person—old, young, hungry, curious. These figures are the images of the actor. They

'WHAT'S MY MOTIVATION?'

are the physical apparitions of his inner state. These images must have function, purpose, urgency. Devote yourself to their needs.

In Jean Genet's *Deathwatch*, Green Eyes, the condemned murderer, is chained to his cell—not *like* a rabid dog, but because he *is* also a rabid dog. Touchstone in *As You Like It* does not bounce on Audrey's lap because he is *like* her yo-yo, but because he *is* also her yo-yo. The art of acting increases by geometric proportions. At first one is a person with a body and a voice and intelligence and an empathetic urge. And then one is coupled with a character with his own body, voice, intelligence, urge. At last one is the metaphor, the extension, of that character. That extension is the leap from the actual to the universal.

6. *Find something you love in every person working in your theatre.* It is the only way to trust, and trust is the only way to achieve the alert abandon that acting demands. If you find your leading man to be unredeemingly unlovable, or if you can barely tolerate the slide projector operator, do not deceive yourself. Your acting will suffer. You will be incapable of giving unreservedly, unresentfully of yourself. Note: You do not have to love these people beyond the hours of warmups, rehearsals, and performance—and often it is better not to.

7. *Find something you love in every character you play.* Love makes you responsible to the character. When you can justify the painful basis of Iago's jealous rage, you can commit yourself to his desperate actions with all your power. When you can relish your purpose at the doorway of a king, you will stand guard against the enemies of both the king and your own significance. "There are no bit parts; only bit players" speaks of the actor who is willing to compromise himself by playing a shadow of a character. Such halfhearted tomfoolery fools no one, least of all the caring actor.

8. *Find something you love on every stage you work on.* You have to want to be there. Seek the promising floorboard or the graceful arc of a leko. Even if you don't get to stand near it, you know it is there. If you don't want to be there, it is unlikely that anyone watching you will, either.

You cannot hide for long what you truly feel. If you are an actor at all, you will communicate those feelings. Acting is not the putting on of a mask. Acting is the revealing of true expression.

9. *Find a way to believe that each member of the audience is your equal.* Share, don't preach. Demand as much of yourself as you expect from them. Give them the full opportunity to see you, to hear you, to recognize your image. And then let them thank you with their applause. It is a surreptitious conceit to deny the audience the right to acknowledge a gift. There are some cases in which a curtain call will feel absolutely wrong; but these cases are truly rare, as rare as genius. And let the audience seek you out in the halls of the theatre, outside your dressing room after the performance. Just as you needed to fulfill the purposes of character, so they need to complete the embrace that you have extended to them.

10. *Find something you love in yourself.* There is little value in following any of these exercises without the comfort of an essential love for yourself. You cannot become someone else. You will always remain you. It is the duality, the coupling of spirit, the blend of you and the character that transforms the page to the stage. And that transformation is what we attend with such hopeful urge. Love yourself, that we may love you.

IN THE THEATRE

Auditions. For the director, the purpose of the audition is to find out as much as possible about each prospective actor in the shortest possible time. For the actor, of course, the purpose of the audition is to get a role. Since the actor is usually unaware of what the director is looking for, as the director often is as well, the best course for the actor is to give the most that he can of himself at each audition, respecting constraints of time and hints of character.

An actor presenting a prepared monologue often displays more about his past roles than his future potential. Rarely can the impact of a full performance be reestablished in a two-minute routine, although intimations of it can sometimes be evoked. A performance is not a lightbulb, to be switched on and off. But a performer is also a technician, and he has an obligation to develop those techniques that can aid him in bringing forward a performance on demand, and under demanding conditions. The brief excerpting of a role is not the optimum basis for the director's decisions about actors, but it is the most common, and may seem to be the most efficient.

Sometimes the person conducting the audition will give the actor-hopeful a script of the play for which actors are being sought. This is called a "cold reading," frequently an apt description. The temptation for the actor seeing these words for the first time is to throw a powerhouse punch of phony attitudes at this paper tiger. It is far better to "talk and listen" (a technical as well as literal term) to the script than to put the cart of emotion before the horse of understanding.

The two-minute audition is necessary, because there are so many would-be actors for so few roles to be performed. But a small theatre can make, if not the best, at least the better of the trial situation that an audition presents. The director can ask a small group of actors, perhaps four or six, to enter the audition space together. Then he can ask for a brief warmup, involving body and voice. The observant director will be able to discern the active choices each actor makes; the extent, nature, and effect of the actor's training; a hundred bad habits; and, most important, the awareness and sensitivity of one actor to another. The director may not wish to tell the actors what he is looking for, lest they try to give it to him. By so doing, they are liable to ignore their own vital instincts. These impulses will provide the pulse of every scene in the play to be. Therefore, director: See what comes naturally. Be alert to the presence of an actor. Before every audition series, read Joseph Chaikin's *The Presence of the Actor*. "The more baffled and astonished we permit ourselves to be," he says, "the more we discover and learn."

If the call for a warmup results only in blank stares from the auditioning actors, you must decide quickly if you want inexperienced actors in the play. No matter what, try to help the auditioner feel good about himself in whatever he does. Suggest that he walk around the space and get to know it, or sing a song and listen to its echoes, or stretch and shake like a cat or a tree. Let him jump with the ropes of his imagination. Tell him that the only true purpose in acting is to have fun.

At the close of this period, while the actors think they are still warming up, the director can ask for a brief improvisational encounter to give the actors a sense of purpose and completion. If this improvisation entails each actor's saying his name to another actor, for some reason, in some way, it can also serve as a mnemonic device for the director who is swamped with petitioners.

You will have used, in this preliminary audition, only two minutes per actor. But each actor will have been working in the space for twelve minutes, and things will have had a chance to develop. Secretly, the director can have been observing for eleven and one-half minutes the one actor who has arrested his glance.

What to do until the genius comes is of considerably less importance for the director than what to do after he arrives. What keeps the director alive at auditions is his willing suspension of disbelief that the genius is ever going to arrive at all. Stay awake. He may enter slouching, trivial. You might miss his moment.

For the actor, the significant phrase in all of the above is *active choice*. Whatever you do, make a decision to do *something*—a task, not a display—and try with all the physical and vocal vocabulary at your natural command to accomplish it. Do not stretch: reach for a palpable blossom. Do not somersault: capture the whirlpool in your stomach. Do not sing: connect your voice to the music of the mountains. It is all right to choose to speak anything, obscure or obvious. Any physicalization is acceptable, so long as it does not interfere with the choice of another person in the space. The significant task for the actor is to make a decision, to have a purpose in each action, to commit himself to carrying it through. Don't worry. If you are fully present at the first audition, you will almost invariably have a chance to read at the callbacks.

Callbacks. The director will call back certain actors for another audition as soon as he has made up his mind whom he wants to see again—which is usually a few days after all the auditioners have given up hope. At the callback, the director attempts to associate particular actors with particular roles in the play to be given. The actor will read from the scheduled play, often with another auditioner. Sometimes, luckily, a partnership develops between them; and, sometimes, unluckily, a competition.

Actors may ask the director at this point if there is anything special he would like to see. But the actor must stay true to himself, even within the restrictions of a director's wishes. The actor may awaken the director to the very thing he has been looking for all along and has been unable to perceive. After all, the real work of the actor is to use all of his being to bring to mind otherwise unthinkable enchantment.

Preparing Your Role. Read the script. Remember what happens. Especially remember what just happened in the scene directly before the one you are rehearsing. Each event in the series of events that form a play alters the character. Each moment in the series of moments in the two hours on the stage alters the relationship between your character and another character. These alterations are called character development: the organic result of one tiny confrontation after another. Everything onstage must be specific, exact, now, here. There are no generalizations. Examine each scene, each change in rhythm, in search of emerging purpose and the manner of achieving it.

Reading books on how to prepare your role does not guarantee that you will become a better actor. It can even damage some actors, who seek to model their own creative instincts after those of a dead professor. With caution, try Konstantin Stanislavski's *An Actor Prepares*, *Creating a Role*, and *Building a Character*; Antonin Artaud's *The Theatre and Its Double*; and Richard Boleslavsky's *Acting: The First Six Lessons*.

Georgia O'Keefe says, "To see takes time, as to have a friend takes time." The actor needs to make a best friend of the character he embodies. It is not enough to like him. That makes the actor proud. The actor must learn to love him. This love makes the actor responsible. Get to know your character with your mind, with your heart, with your fingers, in your dreams. Live for him, at least for those two hours upon the stage. He cannot live without you, and you dare not walk up there without him.

CURTAIN

Rabbi Hillel was the Calvin Coolidge of the Talmudic community. Challenged by a member of his congregation to explain all of Judaism while standing on one foot, the rabbi bent his right knee and said, "Love thy neighbor as thyself. All else is explanation." Then he put his right foot back on the ground.

The actor is the theatre. All else is elaboration.

8 Rehearsal

REHEARSAL IS THE SEARCH FOR UNITY, for simplicity, for the wholeness of the familiar and mysterious world of the play. At rehearsal each actor must nurture his senses: sight, hearing, balance. Each must feel that Jungian passion play of fear, anger, pain, and love embattled in his heart. Each must know the lure of this event, will towards it, struggle against its obstacles.

Each rehearsal must provide a context in which an actor can create. There are many different techniques: improvisation, blocking, double-time, stop and start, run-through, and more. There are as many approaches to plays as there are directors and plays. But each rehearsal must force the actor to discover a little more than yesterday within the limits of the play as the director understands those limits. Physically, vocally, in emphasis or characterization, the actor will occasionally go beyond these limits. He must be permitted these excesses from time to time, for the experience and the knowledge they provide, as well as for the confidence they give that the director will firmly, gently reestablish the proper limits. The actor must believe on every level that the director will keep him on track; will demand from him the best, help him to achieve it, and acknowledge it when he does.

The director must keep each actor physically safe, spiritually vulnerable, and aesthetically eager. Each actor will have his own idiosyncratic locks; the director must be unrelenting in opening them, in prodding the urges that live within the actor's soul. Approval is not the only key. Approval can be dangerous; the actor's ecstasy will come, ultimately, from himself, and outside approval is merely a pleasant extraneous comforter. The director, then, must prevent the actor from becoming dependent on him, lest that actor later become dependent on either the audience or the critic. The actor's self-awareness, not his self-consciousness, is the painful tool that the director is obligated to hone.

The purpose of rehearsals is to achieve a performance, by gaining imagery, insight, and security through repetition. These weeks are spent developing a symbolic language: of sound, verbal and nonverbal; of gesture; of movement; of light. This language will speak of the outward appearance of the characters, the events and encounters that affect them; and it will speak of their inner lives as well, so that their existence is both temporal and transcendent. But do not think too abstractly during rehearsal. Think of this moment, this touch, this work, this glance. Think of the moment just previous; and gradually let the moments expand until there is life. The final run-throughs provide the opportunity to consider the cumulative pattern and effect of that life, to reaffirm that it is one, and complete.

The director must give impetus and impulse to each project. He must have some notion of what he wishes to accomplish at rehearsal each day, but he must be alert to serendipitous discoveries. He must possess an uncanny sense of rhythm, permitting things to roll along when they are rolling in towards the play, and stopping them when they drift away. The director will not be able to see everything before it is realized on the stage; but he must be aware of it once it happens: his stomach must be responsive. The director must help the actors find ways to recapture the truths that pass through rehearsals like puffs of western winds.

Style is the mark the director makes on a particular production. It can be the inventing of convention, or the disfiguring of it. Do not be afraid to examine the old vaudeville routines, the planted exits of nineteenth-century melodramas, asides, song cues, double takes. Know the conventions, and then you will be able to transform them to make those of your own production. You do not have to reinvent the typewriter to write a new poem.

Read George Bernard Shaw's *The Art of Rehearsal*. It is quaint and charming; and if rehearsal is your work, it will make you feel good about going to work in the morning.

Schedules and Timing. Outline a schedule for the six weeks or so that you will be in rehearsal. The first week should be for improvisations, and for getting acquainted with each other and the script. Over the next weeks you will gradually narrow down into the focus of each particular scene. But even within those rehearsals, leave spaces for renewed improvisatory work or for the practice of whatever specific skills—a song, a dance, a pratfall —are called for in the play.

Allow plenty of time for the "put-in," the placing of the set and the hanging of the lights. Schedule two technical rehearsals: one "dry," without actors, and one "wet," with actors. And allow for at least one dress rehearsal.

The best time for a rehearsal is morning, before the other world's day can interfere with that of the stage world. But salaries at most small theatres are such that most actors will have to hold other jobs; so more often rehearsals will be held at night. People are tired in the evening, filled with the day's troubles; rehearsals can seem to come next to last in the priorities of the day. Make every effort to change that outlook. Read *The Dramatic Imagination*, by Robert Edmond Jones; that slim book will make you want theatre to come first.

A rehearsal should not last for more than three hours without a break; though the break should not be so long as to dissipate the atmosphere completely. Jerzy Grotowski and Antonin Artaud can go on all night, or longer; and so can certain workshops in theatre of the extreme. But such rehearsals are for specific experiences of duress, and have their place only with a trained, committed company that has plenty of time and a very patient administrative staff.

Distractions. Eat lightly before rehearsal, and at any break in the middle of one. And do not keep a coffeepot in the rehearsal room. It is not only that the full stomach does not take to physical work; the satiated body does not understand the needs of characters in a play, who must continually redefine their own objectives to keep the action evolving. Make people satisfy their needs onstage, as much as possible. Let the actor be aware every time he has to leave the space to feed some part of himself; such self-awareness is essential. Nothing should be automatic, except the early experiences with the text and the characters themselves.

No actor should smoke while he is rehearsing onstage. To let tension dissolve in the exhalation of smoke is a horrible waste. Smoking can also distort the feelings of another actor towards the character portrayed by the smoker. Halitosis and fog can distance the unsure lover.

Talk as little as possible in rehearsals. The director will need to explain some things, set up others, or give notes, or comments, on what has just happened. But talk can become a substitute for action or an avoidance of it, even when the talk is about the play itself. And talk about other subjects poisons the involvement with the work at hand. Newspapers should be banned from the rehearsal room; they are a constant clutter and a topical distraction.

Visitors should not be allowed to observe rehearsals, unless the acting company and the director agree to it, and then only late in the rehearsal period. Actors must feel free to make fools of themselves. An observer can precipitate a performance before its time; and the actor who leaps to false, invented results can find it extremely difficult to regain his innocence, to reenter the process of fumbling through to results of greater dimension. The unready, ill-formed characterization is necessary along the way, shown only to the trusted director, the reliable stage manager, and the fellow actors who are taking equal risks. The way deserves privacy, respect, and the good judgment of those who guide it.

Notes. The director should give notes to each actor daily. Any actor who has not received a written or spoken comment on an aspect of his work for the day will feel it as a personal affront, or suspect that he has done something irretrievably wrong.

Some notes should be given in front of the whole company of actors and whatever technicians are present. This procedure helps to inure each actor against ego collapse, and forms a bond among them all. But some notes must be given in private, the director alone with the actor; these are usually the ones that other characters ought not to be aware of. Sometimes they involve a touchy acting problem that merits discretion. This privacy and intimacy between actor and director strengthens the bond between these two, who must meld their dreams to make what adequate expression of them that they can. And it helps those actors who must wait for their own notes to learn patience and respect.

Only the director should give notes to the actors. The director knows the play and what he wants to make of it; and the director knows the actors, and where they can best be helped or most easily be injured. Any visitor should give his notes to the director, and let the director decide how to handle them. There are specific circumstances in which an actor might listen to someone other than the director; but such situations are rare, and fraught with the danger of disunity.

The director must often reveal his purpose slowly, as the actors achieve it. General statements about concept and purpose are all right at the opening of a rehearsal period; but too much abstract rumination as rehearsals progress is counterproductive. Actors are not stupid or childish; on the contrary, they may well understand too much and fear that they will never be able to embody it. There is no way to describe everything an actor has to do without making it sound impossible. Do not try. Let the actors find the way for themselves, and they will help the director see far more than he could have begun to describe.

Learning Lines. The memorization of roles will come about in as many ways as there are actors with different ways of working. Some will go home and study a script, covering the words and then checking to see how close they came. Some will associate their lines with a specific area onstage, remembering them only after the blocking is fairly set. Some actors will need to have their roles developed almost completely before they can be "off book," without a script in hand; they need to know precisely and deeply what they are saying, and why. This can be annoying to other actors, and scary for directors who worry about how the late memorizer will gesture with empty palms come performance; but some of these actors are the finest on the stage. Lee J. Cobb, in the original Broadway production of *Death of a Salesman*, sat almost until the first dress rehearsal in a chair with the script in hand, scribbling down the blocking the director gave him. Finally he stood up, carried his chair to the wings, placed his script on it, and entered as Willy Loman: haggard, hopeful, discontent.

Do not feel pressured to have every actor off book at a specified moment, though letting memorization wait until within a week of performance can unsettle the confidence of the entire cast. Allow ample time for the actors to feel comfortable on the set.

No actor should ever "feed" a line to another actor; giving cues is the stage manager's job. An actor can help another actor remember where he is in the script by improvising something "in character," but that must be all. During performance, whispering a line to another actor breaks the bond of illusion between actor and audience. During rehearsal, it makes the forgetful actor lose even more confidence in himself as he sees his partner remember the lines of not only one, but two characters. It presents him with the choice between imitating the actor who has just whispered his lines to him, or trying especially hard to say them differently. It changes the prompting actor from a character onstage into a worried, judging colleague in the mind of the forgetting actor. And, most significant, the forgetful actor misses the chance to discover what he must do to be able to remember the line. He must develop his own memory aids; and often the cause of a lapse is not weak memory but some basic question of character definition. To work through such a problem is worth the struggle.

Ten Bad Habits of Actors. In addition to the prompting of other actors, here are ten of the most common bad habits of potential actors:

1. Whispering.
2. Facing away from the audience, and its extension, closing the eyes.
3. Carrying the head forward of the rest of the body.
4. Posing, especially with one hand on one hip or two hands on two hips. Snobbery is not glamour, and attitudinizing is not acting.
5. Fiddling with objects, clothing, or parts of the body.
6. Looking away from the eyes of the character spoken to.

7. Sarcasm, to give the appearance of intelligent argument.
8. Cuteness, to give the appearance of appealing dialogue.
9. Pointing the index finger at another actor to prove that he is speaking intensely to him; and its extension, shaking that finger.
10. Saying "uh," or its extension, "um," to indicate sincerity. This hesitation is arhythmic and uninformative, and it undercuts the power of the actual words.

Any actor can display a particular bad habit. Note that most bad habits, including those listed here, can be symptoms of avoidance of real confrontation. The actor may be very close to an honest feeling, but fear to grasp it fully. Perhaps the actor who "breaks," or laughs out of character at the wrong moment onstage, is reacting to something funny; but there may be something terrifyingly real on the verge of his consciousness. The director's refusal to let that actor indulge in his habit can be the ticket to the journey of theatrical realization. To usurp these fears with a healthy dose of inspiration, reread *Acting: The First Six Lessons*, by Richard Boleslavsky.

Ultimately the whole show must belong to the actors, who share it with the spectators in two hours of crazed generosity. The actors do everything, except the technical support; the director can only help them approach it. So, director, do everything during rehearsals except to do it for them. Do not give line readings or exact gestures except in the most desperate circumstance. You do not want an imitation of a performance from the actor. You want its creation.

The director must let the actors do as much as they can safely do, and then remove the excess to reveal the essentials. This is far easier than figuring out ways to get the actors to do more than they have done; though this, too, is sometimes necessary. Remember Michelangelo, who said that he sculpted by removing what was unnecessary from the slab of marble; and Artur Rubinstein, who said that his secret in playing the piano was merely not to hit the intervening keys.

There is no such thing as a perfect rehearsal. There is no such thing as the absolute repetition of an experience. There is only one moment followed by another; influencing it; inevitably, surprisingly, making it happen on the stage.

9   Designer and Crew

C ONCEPT IS THE DIRECTOR'S METAPHOR, as he gives
physical expression to his interpretation of the play.
Concept entails the choice of imagery, and the manner of its
realization. When Orson Welles places his version of *Macbeth*
among voodoo tribes, the line between the director and the
designer who shapes his vision blurs. In small theatre, likewise,
the concept is often the thing. Often the most trying relationship
in small theatre, therefore, is that between the director and the
designer.

Because the design is of such importance, and also because
funds are limited in a small theatre, it is likely to be the director
who, with the suggestions of actors, designs her own production.
Unlike the author who directs his own play, the director-designer
runs little risk of actual calamity. The unity of any production
must emerge from the director's mind. But visual artistry can
surely give dimension and definition to her vision. And proper
technique can mean it is easily and cleanly constructed, safe, and
durable.

The designer is both artist and craftsman. The director
assumes final responsibility for everything, including the design

and how it is executed. But beyond that, the small theatre is too small to have much room for hierarchies. The director shares his concept with the designer and craftsman, who will make it resonant and acute. That unguarded sharing is to be fostered.

SETS

The set is the "thing world" of the play. It is meant to be both a reflection of and the sustenance for the "person world" of the play. If the characters are to breathe their lives freely, the set must be open enough to allow that exhilaration. A set is not the same as a photograph. Applause when the set appears is not a sign of anything particular having been accomplished. The purposes of the set are fulfilled only during the course of the action of the play—not before it begins, and not after it is over.

The design is frequently the only nearly permanent aspect of the production. Unlike a performance, which disappears nightly except in memory, the hard, tactile design stands as evidence against the wishful imaginings of a director. "Talent is necessary for the writing of a play," says Nemirovitch-Danchenko, Stanislavski's partner at the Moscow Art Theatre, "but genius for its production." Most probably he was aiming his remark as much at the director as at the designer; but precisely because the set is such unmistakable evidence of the inner life of the play, it dare not belie the genius of concept.

The Vocabulary of the Set. The vocabulary of the stage is as much fun as any other aspect of the theatre. Especially in small theatre—and even more in small makeshift theatre—where so many of these accoutrements have disappeared from use, it is elegant to recite their names:

Legs	Wings	Trap
Teaser	Flies	Revolve
Traveler	Drop	Elevator
Tormentors	Flat	Distemper Color
Apron	Cyclorama	Green room

Legs are the narrow curtains that hang on either side of the stage from above the audience's vision to the floor of the stage, to hide the offstage areas on either side.

Teaser refers to the very wide, short curtain that hangs from above the audience's vision to just below a pipe on which lights are hung, masking that device.

A *traveler* is a curtain that opens from the middle out.

Tormentors are metal-framed panels substituting for legs, usually in the most forward part of the stage.

The *apron* is the floor of the stage extending in front of the major curtain or proscenium arch (the wall of the building in which the hole for the stage has been cut).

Wings are the offstage areas to either side.

Flies refers to the offstage area above the stage.

A *drop* is unframed canvas on which scenes for the play are painted. Drops vary in size, and are hung like a curtain from a pipe in the flies.

A *flat* is wood-framed, painted canvas or muslin. Usually four feet across by eight feet high, it is free-standing, with a brace in the back, which is nailed or screwed to the floor or to a movable platform.

Cyclorama refers to an enormous pale blue or white area made of cloth or cement, which curves across the entire back wall of the stage. On this are projected sunrises, sunsets, slides, and a continual variety of plays of light.

A *trap* is an area on the stage floor that can be opened, into which actors can descend and out of which devils can emerge.

A *revolve* is a platform that turns on the stage. In some theatres, it is actually a section of the stage floor itself.

An *elevator* is a section of the stage floor that can be raised and lowered mechanically.

Distemper color refers to the dry powdered pigment used in making scene paint.

The *green room* is the offstage area where actors wait before their entrances. It is so named not only because of the traditional institutional color of the walls, but also for the color of the actors' complexions as they wait.

Constructing the Set. Lest the designer's mouth water over mechanical possibilities, consider Jerzy Grotowski's Laboratory Theatre in Wroclaw, Poland. For a presentation of *Apocalypsis* he used one electric light, placed in one corner of the floor of a room in which the floor, the four walls, and the ceiling had been painted black. The nine actors wore white drawstring pants and long-sleeved white cotton pullover shirts. The only objects onstage were two candles, one loaf of bread, and a rope. For ten years this theatre has been not only the greatest in Poland, but one of the most influential in the western world—profound, bitter, passionate, and practically without technical wizardry.

There is little correlation between the amount of technical gadgetry and the amount of enjoyment in theatre. It is true, though, that seeing the scenery fall down is as unpleasant and distracting as watching an actor fall down. Though there can be wonder in theatre techniques, do not make pretense to more than you can do well. Read Gordon Craig's *Towards a New Theatre* so that you yourself can come upon his essential line, "The earth is made to dance."

A flat is a piece of canvas, usually four feet by eight feet plus hemming, stretched and stapled over a wooden frame. Put a lot of flats in a line, bracing each from behind with lengths of wood so they can stand upright. "Dutchman" them, adding strips of muslin dipped in "dope," or paste, to cover the cracks where the flats meet. Let the muslin dry. Paint all the flats—and behold a set. Such is the traditional way that three-walled proscenium theatre has been designed for a hundred years or more. It has its place, today as well as yesterday.

The canvases of the flats can be repainted season after season and rearranged, their holes patched with pasty pieces of muslin. Memories of past shows can live in the messages the company scribes on the backs of the flats ("Romeo was here, 1952"). The flats are part of the smell of the greasepaint—but they are no longer necessarily part of the roar of the crowd.

It is difficult to be daring in performance and to have that risk-taking feel an organic part of a unified production, in front of a flat. The flat exclaims "set" to the audience. It is but one dimension, as its name implies; and it has become the scapegoat of phony realism on the stage, and the butt of critics' humor ("Everything about the play was wooden, except the set"). If one of the purposes of theatre is to create the illusion that one is not in a theatre, then other methods of making play worlds are needed. The vital choice may not be the flat one, but the solid, that the set may form an inevitable atmosphere for the real limits of the play. Platforms, cubes, spiral staircases, weavings of hemp, swings, slides, and a thousand and one other forms can be used to make an important, unified world of many dimensions.

A Few Exercises for the Designer. In addition to reading art books, becoming acquainted with periods and styles, learning techniques of simulation, and glancing through the books recommended in the appendix to this book, I suggest patient searchings of your own environment.

1. *Identify the few objects which define a world.* Simplicity is one essential key to theatre design. Look around you. What is the least you need to see in order to know precisely where you are? What seems large, what small, and what do you wish to be close to, or far from?

2. *Examine an object.* What were the events that brought this object to its present state of sheen or disrepair? Who were the people who came into contact with the object, who kept it, who discarded it? An armchair, a teakettle, a typewriter all have a history of intimate contact with real people. If you can learn to respect these objects and the stories they tell, you will be more able to place objects on the stage in a dynamic relationship with the characters of the play.

3. *Transform the object.* Imagination in small theatre is often and happily a necessary substitute for the actual, for both financial and aesthetic reasons. Look again at that armchair. How can it become a throne? Look again at that teakettle. Do you hear it sing, or sense the warmth of its steam? Can that typewriter become an engine that moves language in and out of time? Softly, gradually, ask yourself how twenty feet by thirty feet can contain a world.

4. *Contemplate optical illusions.* What is not there is as important as what is there—and so is the shape and size of all the "not-thereness" of the stage. For most of his time onstage, after all, an actor moves in space, not in contact with walls, furniture, objects. As a designer, try to shift your vision, much as those optical illusions force you to see first one thing, and then the obverse picture. What had been background for one image becomes the significant image, the other but background for it. Perceive your set not as the placement of things, but as a shaped space. Look at the levels of space, at the angles of space, at the

sizes of space. Make of the space, as well as of the things that occupy space, a reflection and an extension of the inner world of the characters who inhabit it.

Coping with Limitations. Because small theatre is small, its budget is severely limited. Exploit poverty. You will not be able to make silk purses out of sows' ears, but you may be able to convince someone that you have. Because small theatre is small, storage space is severely limited. Exploit simplicity. Little strips of Mylar can have many facets, a hundred colors, and a mysterious glow. Remember the adage: There are no problems in theatre, only opportunities.

The temptation may be to use and reuse everything you have. Those flats can be repainted and rearranged. Or you can build some basic platforms using plywood tops and either legs of varying lengths or folding metal frames, which can be purchased at lumber stores. You can build a few sets of stairs of different heights. The configurations of these elements, plus a few objects, dashes of cloth, string, paper, balloons, and more, can shape an infinite variety of sets. But if the same audience returns to play after play, as you hope, they will quickly learn what to expect when the house lights go out and the stage lights go on. They will have seen it all before, in another arrangement; and your challenge will become to let them see it newly each time.

Another choice is to borrow or build inexpensively enough that you can give it back or throw it away without too much nostalgia at the close of the play's run. The audience will not know what to expect from you, except to expect something different at each play. This choice may sound promising. Its drawbacks, however, are twofold. First, everything may end up looking as cheap as it actually was. Second, the designer may strain to be different or clever, at the expense of remaining true, useful, and essential.

The ideal is probably some combination of minimalism and surprise. Keep the play always in mind, and constantly check the picture in your head against the actual one onstage.

Safety. Consider carefully when you build your set questions of the safety and maneuverability of the actors who must move within the space, and of the crew who will have to handle the set.

The small theatre is neither blessed with nor beholden to a large crew—those folks who construct, maintain, and move the pieces of the set from scene to scene. Do not put in more elements of set than your numbers of crew can comfortably handle. The set must not become a burden. It is support for, and one important expression of, a play.

The set must be as safe as our limited awareness can foresee. In theatre, as in most other endeavors, anything that can go wrong will. The chair leg will collapse at the exact moment the heroine touches it. The cigarette lighter will not ignite at the precise moment our hero is demonstrating his suavest machismo. The butler will discover the doorknob in his hand at just the moment he was about to announce the arrival of the mysterious tuxedoed guest. We can only hope that these traditional disasters have their chance to happen before the opening night.

Here are some basic rules for safety on the set:

- Wherever one bolt holds something in place well, add another.
- Sweep the stage thoroughly before each rehearsal and before each performance.
- No one handles a rope with wet hands. If your hands sweat, use baking powder in your pockets or on the rope itself.
- No open flame without water immediately available onstage. No open flame near cloth.
- No frayed cords.
- No cloth that has not been fireproofed.
- No one climbs on any apparatus unless the apparatus is tested nightly. The climber must be trained and confident. There is either an actor as spotter or a mat immediately below the climbing actor.
- No tumbling routines improvised by other than trained tumblers; even then, tumbling should take place on a mat.
- No throwing of hard objects in anyone's direction. Use a soft substitute for the object until aim and timing are refined; or use a marker in place of the actor who is the target.
- In stage combat, the minimum distance from the fictional foe for the thrust of the epee is eight inches above or to the side. In stage combat, unlike in fencing, the object is to avoid striking the opponent.

- Do not fire a stage pistol near the ear of an actor.
- All broken glass must be swept up immediately. If glass breaks during a performance, an actor can enjoy his improvisational skills by cleaning it up then and there.
- Devise a way to lock open all folding furniture.
- All wood must be carefully sanded.
- Stage floors should be nonslip surfaces, and rugs on them secured. If you are on tour and the stage floor is slippery, actors should not wear socks or smooth-soled shoes on it.

Perhaps because the characters they represent are immortal, actors tend to ignore or forget their own fragile mortality. Do not rely only on common sense around your sets. Be uncommonly cautious. And when the inevitable disaster occurs, try not to blame yourself for too long.

LIGHTS

Light allows us to see, and forces us to perceive one thing more sharply than another. It is the light of the stage that permits the primary experience of theatre. Stories have been told, of course, since man found language. But it was only when we were able to see the story form and move that there was theatre. In a theatre building, naturally, there must also be adequate light by which the audience can safely find their seats.

Lighting equipment is expensive. Remember the old stage-hand saying as he pointed skyward: "Look at all the effects He can achieve with only one instrument!" In addition to coffee cans with the tops removed and holes cut in the bottom for the placement of lightbulbs, there are three basic instruments, or *lamps*, which will be useful for the small theatre. In fact, many other instruments will be more detrimental than helpful, as their light spills into unintended stage areas and the eyes of the audience.

The basic three are:

- The *leko*, identified by its L-shape, can be focused. Lekoes come in different sizes, allowing varying focal length, and accommodate different wattage, allowing variations in intensity. When hanging a leko, always remember to keep the end without the bulb above the end with the bulb. Warm air rises, and the bulbless end has a vent for the escape of heat. Every manual tells you this, but every technician forgets it at least once a season.

• The *fresnel* is a square instrument that cannot be focused, but on which barn doors (metal shutter-like leaves) can be slipped to limit the amount of spill. (The shutters in a leko are internal.)

• The *follow spot* needs someone to remain with it in order to operate successfully. Its color changes are internal, and the temptation to use it will often exceed wisdom.

Placement of Lights. To hang lekoes and fresnels you will need *C-clamps*, which can be purchased at any hardware store, and a secure pipe. The general rule for the hanging of lights is to hang them at a 45-degree angle, with equal lighting coming from each side of the stage. This balance "sculpts" the actors, gives them three dimensions, makes them equal. The seductive power of light occurs in the breaking of this general rule.

Color. The traditional colors in stage lighting are achieved by the use of *gels*. A gel is cut from a large piece of colored or frosted plastic and is placed in a frame, which then slips in front of the lens of your lighting instrument. Any gel will decrease the amount of light that an instrument emits.

The gel will be affected by the heat of the light. To minimize the darkening and wrinkling that heat causes in the gel, scratch a new gel randomly before inserting it, using a pizza cutter or a dressmaker's wheel—both common tools in the theatre, where pizza and costumes are equally necessary. This scratching will allow just enough ventilation to prevent the gel from deteriorating rapidly.

The colors themselves are known as *cool* (everything in the blue range), *warm* (everything in the red range), and *frost*, which is colorless and softens glare. Even after years of looking, the lighting designer and the director will still have to look again at the effect of a particular gel before they color a particular actor and his world. The names of the gels imply romance: special lavender, daylight blue, urban blue, flesh pink, surprise pink, bastard amber, straw, flash.

The Lightboard. Lights are operated from an instrument called a *lightboard*, which can be anything from a homemade compilation of rheostat switches to an array of individual and master levers. If a lightboard is not too expensive for your theatre to purchase new, your theatre is not quite so small as you had thought. Any used board is perfectly adequate, unless it lacks an instruction booklet. If this is the case, whoever is to operate the lightboard during the show will have the tremendous responsibility of finding someone who can not only explain everything that can go wrong during a performance but can show how to compensate for any mishaps as well.

Keep extra fuses handy. If the lights go, your heartbeat will probably go too. This disaster—and fire—are the only two mishaps other than personal injury that will legitimately stop the show.

Every city has a book of electrical codes. It is almost impossible for a small theatre not to violate these codes. Have a licensed electrician wire your theatre at the outset, and from play to play do your best to avoid household wiring cords and to keep the inspector from your door. The lightboard operator will enjoy reading basic wiring manuals, and any skill he acquires through this study will certainly prove useful.

Onstage Lighting. There is another source of light, often overlooked; it is from the stage itself. The lamps of the room or the streetlamps in the scene where the play is set; the sparkling of objects that a character handles; flashlights; candles; matches; all of these, and as many more as you sense the need of, can be rich sources of lighting for your play. They do not add mere reality or even the imitation of actuality; they force the spectator to focus on a moment, they demand attention to the explosion of an idea like the lightbulb sketched over a cartoon figure.

Light leads our eyes, and our eyes often lead our thoughts. That lambent guidance can be evoked in many more ways less expensive and more valuable than ever appear in Capron's extensive catalogues.

It is possible to do a play with no set, with only space. But there must be light. And the elements of light—intensity, color, focus—and of its inverse, shadow, are both metaphor and mentor in the world of a play.

SOUND AND OTHER EFFECTS

Recorded and live music and sound effects may all add, even essentially, to the definition of the world of the play. In a small theatre, though, any recorded sound will be recognizable as a recording. Make that recognition work for your purposes and not against them.

Any live music will cost money—not only for the musicians, rented instruments, and insurance, but also because much music carries its own copyright. Permission to perform it can be expensive.

In addition to sound, many other specific arts can contribute to the production. Because the stage is a world, anything at all— except real physical pain—may happen on it that can happen in that other world. This includes all other arts, such as:

- Movies (silent, home, and box-office)
- Videotapes (from television and your own Porta-pak)
- Slides (from trips, the museum, or the very show you are performing)
- Recordings (of symphonies and whales)

Having someone in your theatre with special technical expertise widens your potential symbolic vocabulary, and increases the temptation to use every last word in it. Beware. The stage demands its own unity, its own simplicity, and its own ever-present life. Use only whatever you need, and whenever possible, stay hungry.

PROPS

A prop is to a thing as a character is to a person. To take a shattered Coke bottle and paste it onto painted cardboard, and then to convince an audience that it is indeed the symbol of Edward II's reign, is called *kroveny*.

Despite Polonius, in the matter of props you will often have to be both a borrower and a lender. Because of the probability of damage and loss, the most effective substitute for a precious object should always be used rather than the object itself. You do not need real Spode to drink tea like a lady. You need only to believe, and to communicate that belief. Go to hardware shops, flea markets, dime stores. Seek out the supply houses for restaurants and hospitals. Make friends with factory foremen and service station attendants. Think of the prop hunt as an adventure. It really can be.

When an actor calls, "I can't do this without _____," it may be true. It may also be true that he cannot do it with. Beware the prop that is an unnecessary crutch. And watch out for "being busy"—playing unnecessarily with an object as a substitute for carrying through the real, essential action of a scene.

But props are necessary, and the actor who uses one needs to know where he last left it. The rules about placement of props should be typed, cloned, and posted in prominent backstage areas. And do not let anyone except the actors and crew handle the props of your production.

Props, maybe precisely because they are not real things, become invested with the souls of the actors, who make them more than cardboard, glue, and gilt. Their fragility achieves the symbolism of the delicate structure of a world of spirit and of pleasure.

COSTUMES

Clothes do not make the actor. But they can be his undoing. In case of doubt for a costume, be unobtrusive. The stage is not a succession of Halloweens. The torn sheet, the black cone may make a ghost or a wizard of a child, but that is more because of the charm of the child than because of the costume. The costume, in many ways, is to the character what the set is to the play. It is the place in which the character moves, and which expresses most closely both his inner life and his outward circumstances.

Usually the small theatre cannot afford a costume designer; and the temptation will be great to raid thrift stores or larger theatres' costume shops, or to resort to leotards. The person to turn to instead, to use most fully to discover the right costume, is the actor. He is most intimately connected with the character, and can pull the costume from the wardrobe of the character himself. There is an ecstatic moment, deserved by every good actor, when he can look at himself and say, "Yes. This feels right." That special joy can inform a performance like none other.

With this in mind, provide your actor with as much choice as possible; though it is too much to ask the actor to shop for his own costume at the start. When you go as you must to the thrift store or costume shop, keep in mind both the actor and the character he plays, not simply an idea in your head of "king," or "servant," or "secretary." And return to the theatre with a few costumes for your actor to choose from. Let him improvise the draping of his costume as he tries to place his character inside it. And be silent as the actor feels his way through the clothing you have brought.

Have a good friend in or out of theatre who has excellent sewing skills. Nothing will fit right the first time it is put on; and everything, eventually, will tear. Be circumspect if you construct costumes, especially in small theatre. Such clothing may look more like a costume than like natural apparel. Just as the flat says *set*, the made garment can persistently chant *costume*, reminding everyone that this is "just" a play.

Decide who is to launder the costumes and how often. The laundry schedule should be determined by the frequency of performances and the pores of the actors. It is perfectly reasonable to ask that each actor be responsible for repairing, laundering, and pressing his own costume. And it is perfectly all right to require each actor to hang up his costume neatly after each performance.

At the close of a run, an actor will sometimes want to keep his costume. It is best to wait until the actor asks; but whatever your decision, make it with compassion. Permitting the actor to keep his costume may cause you problems in the future if you should produce the play again or need the costume for another play. But it can also be, for the actor, the only tangible memory of the play to hang in the corner of his closet.

MAKEUP

In a small theatre, the audience is very close in physical space to the actors. Not only will they see that makeup is makeup, but they probably would also be able to see features even if there were no makeup. Rule of thumb: If the makeup is supposed to look like makeup, use it. If it is supposed to be imperceptible, use it sparingly. Besides, greasepaint is exorbitantly expensive. Concentrate your efforts on the acting and the makeup may not be necessary at all. In any case, makeup will certainly not lend credibility to the superannuation of a young and conventionally attractive woman cast in the role of Martha in *Arsenic and Old Lace*. Instead, it may remind the audience continually of the deception they are being asked to believe. Makeup is no substitute for acting.

There are times when it just doesn't feel like theatre without makeup. Makeup is make-believe, a pretty convention. But it can be more. The application of makeup itself—the actor touching his lips, rubbing his cheeks, running his fingers through his hair, coming into physical, sensual contact with himself—is often the beginning of the discovery of his own particular beauty. Insofar as it is relevant, let the makeup reveal that beauty, not mask it.

STAGE MANAGER AND CREW

The stage manager is the right hand of the director until the play opens. But the day that rehearsals end and the play starts its run, the stage manager is fully in charge. It is up to him to see not only that all technical requirements are in good shape and operating well, but also that the performances themselves remain up to snuff. It is often the stage manager who will rehearse an understudy should a member of the cast fall ill or drop out.

During rehearsals the stage manager sits alert to the director, taking notes on everything the actor is asked to do—particularly his "blocking," or where he moves and when during the scene. The stage manager keeps track of all props and costumes needed for the show; checks the safety and cleanliness of the playing area; and keeps an eye on the time.

On performance evenings the stage manager gives time calls to the actors—usually half an hour before curtain, fifteen minutes before, five minutes before, and "places." If your theatre has an intercom, the stage manager will call cues both for the entrances of actors and for the changes of lights, sets, and curtain.

Stage management can sometimes be understood as a training ground for learning something about directing. In this case, it can be a frustrating job; all those tasks that could bring a sense of accomplishment and purpose can bring jaw-clenching annoyance instead. The most happy and the least guilt-inducing stage manager is the one who enjoys the exercise of the duties of stage management.

Remember that it is not the job of the stage manager to provide coffee and cigarettes for the oral gratification of actors whose egos exceed their artistry—and that when these errands must be run, they merit the respect of everyone.

In small theatre the stage manager is often the technical director as well. The technical director would ordinarily be in charge of all the construction of the set, the hanging of lighting equipment, and the pulling together of all the objects necessary for the completion of the stage picture. Even if there is a technical director in a small theatre, usually his presence is temporary, for financial reasons. Sooner or later the stage manager will have to take responsibility.

Small theatres long continually for permanent technical directors, because of the number of things that break, malfunction, and get lost during the course of any run. These small trials and their subsequent complaints encourage us, even force us, to learn just a little more than we would have thought possible.

The stage manager is also in charge of the crew. The *running crew* are those people who move the sets, operate the lights, arrange the props onstage, help with quick changes of costumes during every performance. They do indeed often have to run; but they are called running crew because the things they operate must be in running order. In a small theatre, the running crew generally consist of the same people who constructed the set in the first place.

The people who perform these tasks call themselves "techies." It is a good example of what had been a disparaging word, "technician"—at least in comparison to the lofty "artist"—transformed by pride and humor into a charming and respectful title.

The techie in a small theatre is invariably the least trained of any of those who work there; and, unfortunately, also the most likely to be in physical danger. These are the willing and fearless volunteers that every small theatre needs and rarely can afford to pay. The first rule for a techie, novice and experienced alike, is: *Do not climb a ladder alone in a theatre.* Every techie needs a partner. Two techies are not only better than one; one techie is unsafe, overworked, and abusable.

The crew will probably have to do all building of the set on the stage itself. It is unlikely that the building in which you have rented space will have a shop, let alone a shop that is sound-proofed from the rest of the building. The crew, designer, or technical director may have access to a shop, garage, or basement away from the theatre. In this case, make sure that everything built there fits through the doorway of your theatre!

If all building must be done onstage, allow adequate time for the crew to work there exclusively, without having to avoid actors rehearsing in the space at the same time. Be sure that not all construction time is between the hours of midnight and 6 A.M. —although sometimes, to avoid noise and inconvenience to the others in the building, it will have to be done in those predawn hours.

Folks can be very tired at these times. Companionship and wakefulness are absolutely essential—for safety, for morale, and for satisfactory results.

Technical Rehearsals. Technical rehearsals occur after the actors have rehearsed sufficiently to feel comfortable with their roles, and before the dress rehearsals that immediately precede previews or opening night. At a technical rehearsal, all the technical aspects of the play are gone over and over and over again. The actors are tools during these rehearsals, serving those who operate the machinery of the stage. They are often asked to jump the script from light cue to light cue, or even to repeat the same cue from five to fifty times in order that the lightboard operator feel as comfortable with his role as the actor does with his. Usually, there are only one or two technical rehearsals; and they run longer, and are more exhausting for everyone involved, than any other single rehearsal. Tempers are lost more frequently —and more unjustifiably—at a technical rehearsal than at any other ritual in theatre. But the actor must remember that he has had six weeks to prepare. The technician has only two nights. That actor has, at a technical rehearsal, the opportunity to achieve trouper status, by his display of patience, grace, and generosity in these trying and necessary hours.

10 Performance

WHAT IS IT ABOUT THOSE MOMENTS just before a play begins? What is that expectancy which catches the breath? The house lights dim. A last program rustles closed. Darkness. Hush.

Merde. Break a leg. No whistling in the dressing room. The hexes, charms, amulets of the theatre are cast. The critics have received and responded to their invitations. Members of the company have invited limited numbers of friends, whose complimentary tickets have already been arranged for. All technical equipment—sound, lights, rigging—has been tested. The actors have arrived at the theatre a minimum of one-half hour before performance time. The director has offered an encouraging smile and said, "I'll be enjoying you tonight." Eventually the stage manager calls, "Places, please." Some two hours later the ushers sweep away the halves of tickets left on the floor of the house.

There is only one thing more stomach-wrenching than opening night, and that is the knowledge of the night that follows. With the second night one must relinquish the reckless optimism with which one entered the space the previous evening. The stomach no longer tightens; it shrinks.

IN THE HOUSE

The House Manager. The house manager oversees or runs the box office, where reservations are listed, tickets are purchased, and sufficient change is kept on hand for patrons with bills of large denominations. The house manager has the responsibility for getting the ticketed audience into and out of the theatre accurately, safely, and politely. She engages the ushers and instructs them in their duties. At the close of each performance, or during it, the house manager completes the box office statement.

The box office statement lists the number of people attending, the amount of income for that evening, and any particular

Sample Box Office Statement

Statement by _____ Date _____ Play _____

Payment Mode	Number	Amount	Total
MC/Visa			
Amex			
Cash/Checks			
Vouchers			
Other			
Group Discount			
Comps			
Press			
Other			
Total			
No. of Reserv.			
No. of Subscr.			
No-Shows			
Off-Street			
Extenuating Circumstances			

condition (such as weather) that might have affected the evening's attendance. It is a good idea as well to keep account of the number of reservations, no-shows, and "off-street" tickets (patrons without reservations). This accounting will give the office some notion of how many telephone reservations one can expect to take during the weeks before a given performance. (An example of the box-office statement appears on the preceding page.)

The house manager in a small theatre is frequently a member of the administrative staff. This doubling is financially helpful for the theatre and for the staff member. It also means that the same person who has been taking reservations during the week is greeting the audience at the door. This personal contact makes your box office a friendly place, and the familiarity with names it facilitates can often help ease a difficult situation when someone's reservation has been lost or a complaint is made. Often, the house manager is the only person in your company who will have the real pleasure of greeting the patrons of your theatre at the door.

The house manager sometimes has responsibility for guarding the halls during the performance. It is wise to lock up your evening's receipts away from the entrance the moment the performance begins; though in the case of an intruder, no amount of money is worth the injury of a member of your company. Hand over the money. Fast.

It is the house manager who must keep the hall quiet during the performance and deal with latecomers, as the ushers will have already been seated to watch the play. Of all the jobs in the theatre, house managing once the show has begun can be the most boring. Director, take a turn guarding the hall for the house manager from time to time.

Ushers. Take out classified ads in local newspapers for persons to usher free at your performances. These volunteer ushers will work for one performance. They sweep the house before and after the show, they take and tear the tickets, and they hand out the programs. In exchange, they receive a free ticket to the show. They will also probably want to bring a friend along in a paying seat. The theatre thus gains both audience and important help for the price of an inexpensive ad.

Ushers should be clean and pleasant. Sometimes the person who arrives to usher will be dirty and unpleasant. It is perfectly all right for the house manager to say she doesn't need an usher tonight; but give the person a free ticket anyway. He arrived with that expectation. It takes a lot of free tickets to equal the cost of an argument while an audience is walking into your theatre.

Timings. The usual run of a single show in a small residential theatre is six weeks. Performances generally take place Wednesday through Sunday evenings, although if the theatre is located in a church Sunday nights are frequently off limits.

One of the advantages of a small theatre is that even if attendance is small, you can continue running a show that you believe in. So whatever length run you initially decide on, it is a good idea to sustain it. If there is enough audience demand, or if by some unforeseen circumstance your next show is not quite ready, you can even extend it.

A seven o'clock curtain is useful if you plan on having a late show the same night, usually at nine-thirty or ten o'clock. Friday and Saturday are the only nights on which a late show is worth the additional effort it requires.

If you are planning a single performance each night, keep the curtain time consistent—say, seven-thirty or eight o'clock. If on any particular evening you must change the time of the curtain, make it later rather than earlier. Latecomers disturb the performance and the other members of the audience; and they will also spend the rest of the evening trying to figure out how much and what they have missed.

Latecomers are always admitted at the discretion of the theatre. It is the director of a play who sets the rules on the timing of their admission, and the house manager who carries out those rules. Warn the actors before the performance if you will be admitting latecomers, and if they will be admitted at one particular point in the performance or can be expected to trickle in throughout the first twenty minutes of the show.

In a small theatre most seating will be unreserved. The audience is guided to the seats on a first-come, first-served basis. This makes it possible to leave empty a block of seats near the entrance to the house, thus causing as little disturbance as possible when latecomers must be seated. This convenience will please the latecomers, who generally have no wish to attract attention.

Even if you have subscribers who have been guaranteed particular seats as part of their subscriptions, you can say in print that these seats will be held only until five minutes before curtain time. The subscriber is the one member of the audience who may be distressed at being seated on the side or to the rear. Remain kind, calm, and firm.

Despite the probability of a few latecomers, try to start the show as close to the appointed time as possible, with reasonable consideration for parking problems and delays caused by weather. Both the acting company and the audience can be trained to be prompt, although both will have access to limitless excuses for delay.

An average show lasts up to three hours. If it is less than one hour long, the audience will feel cheated. If it is more than three hours, you had better announce this on the program; the subways may stop running, or the babysitter may have a curfew. Also announce on the program if there is to be no intermission, and say if there are one or two intermissions. It is difficult for an audience to remain comfortable in their seats for more than an hour and a half without an intermission, unless the performance truly rivets them there.

Discounts and Complimentary Tickets. In addition to free tickets for members of the press and friends of the company, and discounts for subscribers and groups, there will be occasions on which you will want to offer discounts to the general public. Be fair; be prudent. A discount will not necessarily increase your ticket sales. Do not penalize patrons for buying tickets in advance at the full price. If you have sold ten tickets to your hundred-seat house at full price, and you wish to offer the remaining ninety at half price, you must compensate the original ten. You can offer them a bonus of additional tickets, or give them premium seating. Avoid refunds as much as possible. Your theatre may already have spent the money anyway. Only if your patron with the advance sale ticket is from out of town and cannot possibly use a credit for your next show should you give him a 50 percent refund.

Do not try to pass tickets out surreptitiously to friends at the box office. Nothing escapes the eye of the patron with his hand on his wallet; nor should it. Complimentary tickets for friends must be arranged and approved in advance, and should be ready at the box office in an envelope with their names on it.

The number of complimentary tickets allotted to each company member merits careful consideration. You want some audience for each show, especially for "slower" nights; and you also want to offer some perquisites to theatre workers, who are certainly underpaid. But each free ticket diminishes the nightly income. A fair number to settle on is four free tickets per person for the entire run of each show, with an extra two for opening night. You can reasonably ask that complimentary tickets not be used at Saturday night performances.

If the theatre sets a firm complimentary ticket policy, those who work in it are freed from the obligation of deciding how to say no to many friends. They can truthfully, and cheerfully, blame the theatre and absolve themselves.

Programs. Every play must have a program; consider yours carefully. It will be the first encounter a member of the audience has with the play, and it may be the only thing he takes home from the theatre. If you find many programs torn to shreds, chewed up, and strewn underneath the seats, you have a pretty good idea of what the audience thought of your play. If, on the other hand, there is not a program left in the house after the show, smile. They will remember you.

The program should list, in approximately this order, the title of the play, the author, the director, the cast, and the designers and technical staff. The administrative staff of the theatre as a whole can be listed either after the specific production company or on another page of the program. You must also acknowledge public funding sources on the program, and you may wish to thank private benefactors here as well. For everyone listed on the program, check carefully the spelling of names and the designation of jobs.

The names of actors can easily be presented in order of appearance. If two actors enter together, the one who speaks first is listed first. "George Spelvin" or "Georgina Spelvin" is the name used by an actor or actress who is doubling in a role for which a secret identity is desired: an Agatha Christie surprise, for example; or when the mayor of your city is also a closet actor; or when you are embarrassed by the small size of your acting company.

The director who lists his name at the bottom of the program is indulging in false humility. It should not be permitted.

The substitution of an understudy deserves prominent announcement at the box office when tickets are purchased, and either by someone speaking to the audience just before the curtain or by a notice in the program. Sometimes a member of the audience will demand a refund because an understudy is appearing. Within reason, try to avoid refunding any money; offer a credit towards another performance. But if the person insists on his money back, give it to him. Someone who leaves your theatre angry probably will not return; but someone who feels he has been treated fairly may.

An important question that will arise is whether to sell advertising space in the program. There is no right answer. Advertisements will yield some income for the theatre, and the seeking of ads will generate some publicity about the coming performance. But any commercial message may be antithetical to what you hope is happening onstage. Think carefully before you decide to tell your audience about a delicatessen first and your production second.

A program can also contain program notes. These notes should say something extra that relates to the play: biographical information about the author, for example; or a discussion of the translation; or a reference to the historical context of the events. Do not judge or defend the play in the program. The play is obligated to explain itself, and you need not begin on the defensive. But an audience will delight in garnering little-known facts. Offer them. They will help to quiet a restless audience should something unforeseen delay the start of a show.

Audience Behavior and Comfort. Make your audience as comfortable as possible without encouraging naps. It is hard, except in children's theatre, to forbid food in the house; and it is impossible to prevent every piece of hard candy from being wrapped in crinkly cellophane. You can risk an unwelcoming impression with stern signs and severe glances; or you can try a little humor in your requests. But do not expect perfect obedience from your audiences even though they expect perfect perform-ances from you.

Coughing in an audience is a clear sign of boredom. There is only the minutest chance that it is bronchially induced. The sign of sleep, one must remember, is that the sleeper does not swallow. As a member of the audience begins to doze, saliva begins to collect in his throat. Eventually, if you do not hear him snore, you will hear him cough.

On those lucky nights when there are more members of the audience than seats in the house, you can either stand the over-flow at the rear or seat them on the floor at the front. This crowding generates its own excitement and can spark new inten-sity in the performance. But in your pride at attracting so many patrons, do not let the theatre become so crowded that no one can enjoy the show for the elbow in his ear.

Actors, director, and playwright will have to resist blaming the audience for the lack of success of any one night's perform-ance, moaning that the house was too small, too inattentive, too insensitive, too uneducated, overeducated, cold, or hot. You may then be forced to give them all the credit when the play goes well—when you know perfectly well to whom that credit belongs. It is your job to exhilarate an audience, not the other way around.

You will perform a play many times; but each member of the audience will probably see it only once. Commit yourself equally to each performance. A brilliant performance will hold its luster before an audience of ten or twenty times ten. The depth of its effect on any one member of the audience will not be affected by the number of other people who are there to see it.

Curtain Calls. Curtain calls are absolutely essential. It is arrogant or cowardly not to permit an audience to thank you or boo you. Actors should avoid holding hands or embracing during a curtain call. You are acknowledging the audience, and they you. You are not there to display your love for your fellow actors. The curtain call should be an inclusive gesture, not an exclusive one.

If an understudy has just performed, especially if it is for the first time, the other members of the cast may certainly join the audience in applauding him.

Authors take curtain calls; conductors and musicians do; technicians sometimes do, usually from their sound or light booths. But directors never take curtain calls. Directors get their names at the top of the program instead. The applause is for the performance. Once the performance begins, the director has relinquished his claim on it.

BACKSTAGE DURING THE PERFORMANCE

Nobody goes backstage from one-half hour before the performance until after the show is over, except the actors and the running crew. Actors must be quiet while offstage, so as not to interfere with the sounds onstage, and also to allow other actors their moments of preparation.

Most small theatres do not have, and do not need, an intercom system. Cues for lights and sound can be obtained by seeing the stage; and actors can usually hear their own cues for entrances. In large houses, the stage manager "calls the show," or gives the cues, by an earphone system to the technicians and by a paging system to the actors. You may encounter such a system when you go on tour.

For some actors, being offstage during a performance is different only geographically from being onstage. This continuing life of a character must be respected by others and cherished by that actor. Other actors, especially directly before their first entrance onstage, experience a phenomenon commonly known as "stage fright." Some excess of energy, which is probably essential to the actor's transcendence but feels lethal in everyday life, attacks the stomach and the surface capillaries, causing nausea, colitis, pallor, trembling, sweat, and the feeling that death is preferable to this ill ease. Do not pay attention to syndicated news stories offering chemical palliatives. As the Zen master learned, turn to chase the tiger in your dreams. You will ride him furiously.

In general, nothing should go on backstage that does not bear direct, necessary relation to what is going on onstage during that performance. This ban includes talking, eating, drinking, writing, reading. It is true that the cast of *Hamlet* at the Royal Shakespeare Company in London keeps a poker game in progress during all five acts of this monumental tragedy. Such is their tradition; but you had best involve yourself with the practice of your art before the practicing of a tradition.

UNDERSTUDIES

The understudy's appearance onstage, in a small theatre, is usually a last-minute event. You will certainly not be able to pay an actor to be on call throughout a run; and so it is best if there are two people on your theatre's staff already—one male, one female—who can serve as emergency understudies. If these are people who have to be available at performances for another reason, they will be well acquainted with the show. These two staff members may not be the best choices of actors, but they will be convenient, and they will understand the importance of keeping the show going. Their loyalty to the theatre itself may exact from them better performances than you, or they, would

A pill to cure stage fright?

Associated Press

DENVER—Performers suffering the agonies of stage fright may get relief from an inexpensive pill that doctors say works without slowing or distorting the senses.

The medicine, propranolol, is a prescription drug used widely for certain heart ailments. It blocks the flow of adrenalin into the bloodstream, according to Dr. Charles O. Brantigan, director of the Noninvasive Vascular Diagnostic Lab at Presbyterian Hospital.

Brantigan, his brother, Tom, a music instructor at the University of Nebraska, and Dr. Neal Joseph, a professor of ophthalmology, first tested the pill on musicians in Nebraska in 1979.

Their initial research was reported in the Rocky Mountain Medical Journal in 1979. Since then, the team has conducted more tests at the University of Nebraska and the Juilliard School of Music in New York City.

"A performer, beset by fear, finds his body reacting as it would when facing a hostile mob or a tiger," Brantigan said. "Blood is diverted. The heart rate increases, and the increased sympathetic tone causes tremor and a decrement in fine-motor coordination."

During tests at Juilliard, 16 musicians received either the pill or a placebo 90 minutes before each of two test recitals during a two-day period, he said. The musicians' blood pressures were measured before and after each recital, their heartbeats were monitored, and they were observed for outward signs of stage fright.

The tests showed that musicians who took propranolol were less nervous and anxious, had fewer tremors, and perspired less, thereby improving their accuracy, style, and ease during the performance.

have dreamed possible. Try never to cancel a performance. Audiences have little faith in the professionalism of small theatre to begin with. You only reinforce their suspicions by not giving promised performances.

The understudy may have almost no time to rehearse before going on. Do not try to jam a hundred things into her head at the final hour. Probably the most important advice the director can give the understudy, if she does not have the role memorized, is *do not lose your place in the book*. If the role is memorized, the most important advice is *remember: someone will help you out if you forget*. Other actors, help her out. After the initial outing, if there are to be subsequent performances, rehearsal time must be provided for the understudy. It is best if the director can rehearse the understudy privately, and consider her now no longer a mere substitute for an actor, but the actor herself. She is.

ONSTAGE

The paradox of the performance is that it is at once the most public act and the most intensely private. We hear the words; we watch the gestures; and yet what we really confront is the intimate inner monologue that whispers unutterably against our irregular heartbeats. The union between the performer and the spectator is invisible and breathtaking at its best; and when that union fails, the betrayal is overwhelmingly sad.

What is the heritage of two or three hours of people connected without touch? Where do delight and revelation live tomorrow?

11 Publicity

THE PUBLICITY DIRECTOR, who will handle paid advertising, free publicity, and subscription campaigns, has the scariest job in the small theatre. Stage fright is nothing compared to the decision to spend your next-to-last dollar on a newspaper ad, gambling that the money spent will come back in. The publicity director must be a master of the succinct phrase. He must have an acute visual sense. He must respect and enjoy the press corps, thrive under deadlines, and be able to cook under the heat of pressure. The largest calendar in the theatre belongs over his desk. Because so much money is involved, his decisions on size and placement of advertising are made in consultation with the general manager; but it is the stomach of the publicity director that will churn the most.

The publicity director will often find himself in direct conflict with my charge to open the theatre quietly to avoid antagonizing the community. As a general rule, however, he should resist the temptation to promise more than the theatre might deliver. Let the audience discover the excellence of the theatre's work, and the critics spread the praise; especially at first, they will be far more credible than you. An audience will rightfully resent the new company that prances into its community to bring culture to the deprived, especially if what ends up on the stage is a contrived cliche.

One should not open the theatre so quietly, of course, that no one knows you are there. People have to know about you in order to come to your theatre; and they should have the sense of an exciting event about to take place. The publicist must think of himself as the spreader of good news, and act on the faith that there are people who will be eager to respond to it. The moment the word of your theatre's work stops going out, the audience will stop coming in.

There can be nothing more insulting to the publicist than the conceited claim by the artistic staff that audiences have come to their show by "word of mouth." Some, indeed, may have come because a friend recommended the performance. But it is publicity that makes word of mouth concrete, and the publicity director deserves continual credit for his part in making the theatre a part of the community's consciousness.

The publicity director should keep at hand several copies of the theatre's written statement of purpose. He will be its most frequent editor, slanting it for the purposes of each promotional technique he uses.

A sense of humor is also a prerequisite for the publicist's job, which involves continual nudging and nagging both in and out of the company. He will have to pursue members of the company for biographical information to place in news releases, and for information about the production itself. He will have to urge critics to attend, reporters to cover events that relate to the theatre, and advertising departments to give good placement to the theatre's ads.

The underlying rule that the publicity director should impress on each member of the company is that *no one say anything negative about the theatre* to anyone who does not work there. Anything bad that is said by a theatre member to an outsider will be considered by the hearer to be honest, and its effect will last forever. Anything good a theatre member says, on the other hand, may well be thought of as merely public relations. To a large degree, theatre members should let the plays speak for them, and the critics do the judging. Without being aloof, they should answer what questions they can answer positively, and compliment the ones that they cannot.

Press Lists. The first acquisition of the publicity director must be press lists. These consist of the names and addresses of every reviewer and advertising manager at every newspaper, magazine, and radio and television station in the community itself, in nearby large cities, and at local colleges and universities.

Acquiring and regularly updating these lists is a vital chore. It is best if the publicity director can commit to memory the names of each press person and where she works. If the press person believes you care about her, perhaps she will give equal care to your concerns.

There may be an arts council in your community that already has a good press list. There may be another theatre, orchestra, or museum that is willing to let you copy its list. Or you may have to use the telephone directory, and start phoning and asking. It takes hours, but the hours are worth taking.

For mailing purposes, you will need to type names and addresses onto master label sheets, which can then be photo-copied and affixed to envelopes or brochures. It soon becomes clear why the administrative staff is in more danger of unchecked growth than any other area of the theatre. Do not overwork yourself to the point of ill health, but try not to add a new person at each new chore. Remember: everyone deserves payment, and funds in a small theatre are necessarily limited.

From time to time the publicity director will want to put special advertising or promotional emphasis on, or "target," a particular segment of the population. Annotating your mailing lists for this purpose can be helpful in certain cases, especially the subscription campaign (see pages 126–127). Remember, though, that it is very difficult to get most people to the theatre. For the majority of your promotional efforts, to limit your audience unduly to people who listen to a classical music station or people who take one college curriculum is foolhardy.

The Photographer. The publicist's right-hand person is the photographer. There is a special art to being a photographer for the theatre. An actor is best captured as he is living through a moment on the stage. The architectural photographer may be awe-inspiring in his rendition of still marble in the sunset, but absolutely incapable of clicking the shutter in the face of the changing events on the stage. Allow a substantial sum in your budget for the costs of photographs, and find the photographer who works well in such a volatile environment, even if he will not accept point-system payment.

The publicity director should schedule ample time for the "photo call," when the company, preferably costumed, will move repeatedly through scene after scene while the photographer contorts his way among them. Posed pictures do have a purpose, especially in certain plays, but they should not be the only record of your production.

The director should have in mind several scenes to be photographed, being careful to include everyone in the acting company at one time or another. It can be helpful if the photographer has already seen a run-through of the play. He will have ideas on what will work best in a still photograph, which may not be the same thing that works best in motion on the stage. Let the photographer, with a fast film and a willing spirit, set the rhythm for his shooting. Let him call for repeats, and for "freezes." He is an artist, too.

The publicity director will not want to use every picture of every person, but an actor may want a photograph of himself. It is reasonable to ask actors to pay for any photographs they want for themselves; they can make those arrangements directly with the photographer.

Photographs are useful in almost every aspect of the publicist's work. They should be included in the press kits given to every critic who comes to see the show. They can accompany press releases and public service announcements. They can be used in making up posters and display ads. And they can hang in your lobby, as a record of past and present productions. Every photograph must be accompanied by clearly labeled credits, either attached to the back of the print when it is given to the press, or in a separate title when the photograph is posted. The names of the persons in the picture should be listed in the credit, as well as the name of the show in which they are appearing and the name of the photographer who took the picture.

Sample Photo Backing:

WOODMERE THEATRE COMPANY
PRESENTS
''THE WHITE DEVIL,''
BY JOHN WEBSTER
DIRECTED BY SHEILA BROWN

Vittoria Corombona (Jean Williamson) defies Brachiano (Richard Johnson) during her trial in Act III of ''THE WHITE DEVIL,'' as presented by the Woodmere Theatre Company, One Dupuis Lane, Lakeside, New York, Wednesday through Sunday at 8 p.m. through March 20.
Photo by Sherman Whitman.

A photograph should capture the essence of the play. It should make you long to hear the voices of the persons in the picture; it should invite you to share in the event that is cropped in the chiaroscuro before your eyes.

PAID PUBLICITY

There are two kinds of publicity: the kind you pay for, and the kind you get free. The publicity director handles both, and does not live long under the delusion that the latter is any substitute for the former.

Newspapers and Magazines. The major medium the small theatre should use for paid advertisements is the local newspaper. More people will come into contact with you through the newspaper than through most other ways put together; and the printed ad is more enduring than the broadcast one. Find out if your newspaper gives special rates to nonprofit organizations; the money saved can be substantial. And plan your advertising budget at the start of the season; you can often save money by contracting for a number of ads throughout the year.

Be sure to get an answering machine or service for the phone number advertised before placing the ad. It is difficult enough to get someone to call for tickets or information once; twice is almost unthinkable.

Here is the essential information your advertisement must contain:

- *What* (the name of the play and its author at the least)
- *Where* (the name and address of the theatre)
- *When* (dates, performance times, length of run)
- *Telephone number* (of the place to call for reservations)

Any other information in the ad—a photograph, quotations from critics, special rates for groups—can either be a help or a clutter, depending on the size and design of the ad itself. A false impression of a play can be almost impossible to overcome. Trying to alter a viewpoint later can be as expensive for the theatre as it is confusing to the public. If you think no one notices your ads, you will quickly be brought up short by the effect of that misleading one.

Either to represent the theatre or to stand for an individual play, you may consider using a *logo* in the ad. A logo is a symbolic design; it can be abstract or pictorial, made up of a word or an anagram. The logo makes your theatre easily identifiable. On the other hand, your plays will not all be identical, and you do not want to give the impression that they are.

Each play, of course, can also have its own logo. It is amazing how difficult it can be to create in graphic shorthand the essence of a play. Avoid anything starkly ugly, even if the theme of the play is man's inhumanity to man. But do not be ridiculously cheerful merely to attract an audience to a serious play. Create a logo that bespeaks the play, or else use a legible typeface and let it go at that.

Do not use the phrase "smash hit" in an ad. The only thing worse than a cliche is a cliche that implies violence.

As the play nears the end of its run, announcing "Final Three Performances" (or whatever number) may spur the dilatory to your theatre.

Quoting a review in an ad can be effective. But avoid quoting "a member of the audience"; the implication is that there were no reviews worth quoting. And do not take a favorable phrase out of the context of a bad review.

A photograph in an ad can catch a reader's eye. But use one only if you can afford a large enough ad to make the photo recognizable.

Put the name of the play in bold letters. If the author is more famous than the title, put that name in bold letters also. Most

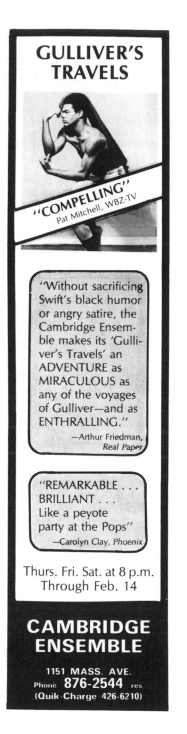

essential, the *phone number* of the box office should be in bold type. Make it easy for the public to know how to reach you.

Try to have your ads prepared "camera-ready" to submit to the newspaper. This means that you have the ad designed, set into type, and pasted up, either within the theatre or by a graphic designer outside the theatre; all the newspaper needs to do is to photograph it for its coming edition. If you are able neither to do this yourself nor to pay someone else to do it for you, be prepared for the newspaper to omit a random line of copy every once in a while, and to misinterpret your instructions on boldness of type even more frequently. There will probably be one newspaper in your area, though, which has a particularly fine ad layout department. If you let them interpret your penciled layout for an ad in their paper, you can then use the printed ad as camera-ready copy for other newspapers as well.

One pleasing visual effect can be achieved by "screening" an ad, which makes the background of the ad appear grey because an even pattern of small black dots has been imposed upon it. (Ask for a 10 percent screen for a light shade of grey, or 20 percent for a slightly darker shade.) This shading will separate your ad from others on the page without giving the funereal impression and the poor legibility of a "reversed" ad, with white lettering on a black background.

A fairly bold border around your ad will set it off from the other ads on the page. Remember, too, that *placement* on the page itself is often more important than the size of the ad. Cultivate the friendship of the person who is responsible for the layout of ads in the newspaper; it is far more useful to court him than to court the critics. You want your ad to be placed at the top of a block of ads, where it will adjoin the editorial copy of the newspaper page. It is far simpler to read in that position than in the midst of a confusion of other ads. If your ad is designed as a reverse, ask that it not be placed next to another reversed ad; they will become indistinguishable in the eye of the reader.

If your community has a daily paper, and if you can afford it, you should place an ad on each day you have a performance, and perhaps one in the Sunday edition as well even if you are not performing on Sunday. People often go to the theatre at the last minute, and they will need to see your name when they check the entertainment page over dessert. Many people will save the Sunday arts section to refer to throughout the week.

Display ads in magazines are more expensive, and they are often too infrequent to be of much help in attracting an audience. Use them judiciously, to reach special audiences such as teachers who might bring groups to the theatre when you are presenting a play of particular academic interest. More general magazines are most useful for their *listings*, which are free of charge (see pages 120–121).

Be sure to have indicated on the large calendar near the publicist's desk the days and times by which ad and listing copy is due at each publication. And get it there on time.

Television and Radio. Television advertising is extremely expensive. The only times that the small theatre will be able to afford it will be those periods when hardly anyone is watching the tube. I advise sticking with public service announcements (see pages 124–125) for all television publicity. And do try hard to get the television critics to your theatre.

Radio advertising is more nearly affordable, but its benefits are uncertain. It is far easier for a listener to miss a thirty-second spot on the air than it is for a reader to miss an ad in the daily paper. The printed ad can be cut out and posted near the phone to call later. Even if a listener does attend to the radio ad, it is unlikely that he will have paper and pencil handy to write down your telephone number, especially if he is driving a car at the time. Radio is a good reminder, but it should not be your primary advertising medium. Be sure, however, to invite radio reviewers to your plays. Reviews on the radio often run several times a day, and last longer than most ads you could consider purchasing.

Posters. The poster is more an art form than an advertisement, less a way of bringing in an audience than a way of beautifying the environment. There is already an effluvia of litter on the walls of your community. Your contribution can be either another eyesore or a vigorous contrast. A poster is a reminder that the theatre exists. Often torn down within hours of its having been put up, it is useful only as an addition to other sources of information and cajolery.

Find a graphic artist who knows and loves your play and

whose fee is not exorbitant. Make certain that the basic information (what, where, when, telephone number) will be on the poster, and then let her create her own art. (You may want to make some prior arrangement for review or revision of the work.) Remember: the poster is usually done before the play opens, so only general quotations from critics about your theatre's work can be included.

Putting up posters will be the shared onus of members of the theatre; and although they may be happy to tack one up in the neighborhood laundromat, long hours spent posting placards in alien byways are less enjoyable. You might want to look into the fees of a poster service at a local college or university.

The poster may not bring anyone to the theatre immediately. But people may take them from their billboards and tack them in their kitchens; unintentionally, they will initiate a priceless familiarity with your theatre. Someday they may even come to see a play of yours, and without knowing why they will sense themselves comfortably at home in your presence.

Flyers. The flyer, or hand-out, is the inexpensive sheet advertising your show that can be passed out to people on street corners or in lines, or left on the shelves of grocery stores or bookshops. This technique can be intrusive, and is often no more than the small organization's contribution to littering the landscape. But flyers do have their purpose; they save the potential audience member from having to write anything down or clip anything out.

Often a flyer will offer a special bargain, such as two tickets for the price of one. If you offer such enticement be sure you are not penalizing those who may have already purchased tickets at the full price. (See page 103 for more on this dilemma.)

Typed and photocopied on letter-weight paper, the flyer offers the temptation of frugality to the publicity director. But keep in mind that you will be placing in the hands of the public a very clear impression of your theatre. Avoid giving a casual, careless, and grasping appearance to the piece that you design. In a similar way, the appearance, behavior, and thoroughness of the people you engage to distribute the flyer will reflect directly on your theatre.

Gimmicks. At first glance it can seem amusing and clever to offer giveaways and related events together with performances of your play—dinner-theatre combinations, for example, or the raffling of bicycles and baked goods. But the dinner may be tasteless, the bike impossible to assemble, the patron diabetic. You may also need a license from your town to offer any sort of raffle; it is often considered a form of gambling. Instead of gimmicks, focus on the play, and hope that your audience will focus on it as well.

Benefits—dances, banquets, parties to raise money for your theatre—will bring persons only to the party, not to your plays. On lucky occasions, you will raise enough to cover the cost of the benefit itself. The appropriate reason to plan a benefit for your theatre is that you want to have a party, not that you want to build an audience. If you do want that benefit, however, remember the play is still the thing; and the attendant publicity for any benefit should eloquently point that out.

Your theatre may sometimes want to participate in a benefit for another organization. Do so for them, not with the thought that it will help you. And after that event, be aware that you may be thought of as a limb of that other body, if you are remembered at all.

FREE PUBLICITY

The four main sources of free publicity, in order of importance, are:

- Listings
- Press releases
- Public service announcements
- Newsletters

All of these cost you something to generate. The first three will be accepted for publication or broadcast by the media at no charge. The last is mailed to subscribers, and left in conspicuous locations for others to take home.

Listings. Newspapers, magazines, radio and television stations, and in-house publications of service organizations will all publish listings of activities in their communities; and it is here that the extra-large calendar over the publicist's desk attains its status.

Every publication and broadcast station has a different "lead time"—the period after the listing copy is submitted and before the announcement takes place. Get those listings in on time. Even more than a display ad, a listing is often clipped from a publication by the avid entertainment seeker looking for an array of weekend choices. And being listed on the air lends validity to your theatre even though you might not advertise through radio or television.

Look at the listings of other theatres, and check with the person in charge of listings, to see how much copy will be accepted. Do not send in too much, lest one of the four necessities—what, where, when, phone—be cut inadvertently to save space or time.

Sample Listings

THE DOCK BRIEF AND THE CHINESE RESTAURANT SYNDROME. One-act play at the Rivertree Theatre, 1629 Platte 433-9216. Opens April 3 for an open-ended run.

THE FANTASTICKS. Musical at Bo-Bans Cabaret at the Bonfils, E. Colfax and Elizabeth, Thurs.-Sat. May 15-June 27. 8 p.m. Also May 17, 8 p.m. 322-7725.

FIDDLER ON THE ROOF. Musical at Boulder's Dinner Theatre, Feb. 11-May 3, 55th and Arapahoe, Boulder, 449-6000. Thurs.-Sun. show 8 p.m., dinner earlier. Sun. show 2 p.m., dinner beforehand.

GILBERT AND SULLIVAN EVENING. Produced by Rick Seeber at Gabriel's Theatre in the Sky, Holiday Inn 1475 S. Colorado Blvd. Wed.-Sun., Sun. matinee. March 11-May 3. Performances preceded by dinner. 759-1616.

GREASE. Musical at Bonfils Theatre, Thurs.-Sun. through May 30. E. Colfax and Elizabeth, 322-7725.

JOKES FOR SPRINGTIME. One-Acts by Chekhov April 30-May 24 at the Germinal Stage Denver, 1820 Market, 572-0944.

A LITTLE NIGHT MUSIC. At the Heights Theater, Loretto Heights College, 3001 S. Federal. April 23-May 2, 8 p.m. 936-4265.

MAD DOG BLUES. Sam Shepard's play at the University of Denver Theater, E. Evans at S. University Blvd. 8:30 p.m., April 23-25, May 12; 2 p.m. April 26, 7:45 April 29-30. 753-2518.

MAN OF LA MANCHA. At Ninth Street Park Theatre, 1111 W. Colfax, Auraria, 629-3403. Opening April 16.

THE OCTOPUS. El Teatro de la Experanza from Santa Barbera, CA, at the Denver Center Space, 8 p.m. May 6-7. 1050 13th, 893-4200.

OFFENDING THE AUDIENCE. Peter Handke's work May 1, 2. 492-7355. Theatre 300, University Theatre, CU.

THE PRICE. By Arthur Miller by the Nomad Players, 1410 Quince, Boulder. 443-7510. April 24-26, May 1-3, 8-9, 8:30, 7:30 p.m. Sun.

RHODE ISLAND FEMINIST THEATER. Presents Paper Weight, a work centering on life at the office, April 30, 8 p.m., Glenn Miller Ballroom, CU.

Press Releases. Contrary to popular opinion, reporters do not generally cover theatres. Theatres cover reporters, with stories about themselves written and submitted by the publicity director. The best press release is one that reads like a news item, not like a story a theatre has planted to compliment itself.

Keep those releases coming. The first ones, of course, will be about the opening of your play; that is a legitimate news event. Later ones can contain personal tidbits about members of your company, or coincidences that relate your theatre with other

Sample Press Release
(to be printed on letterhead stationery)

Woodmere Theatre Company
One Dupuis Lane   Lakeside, N.Y. 92145   332-027-1960

NOVEMBER 15, 1982
FOR IMMEDIATE RELEASE, PLEASE

WOODMERE THEATRE ANNOUNCES THIRD PRODUCTION

LAKESIDE, N.Y.—The Woodmere Theatre Company today announced plans for its next production, Aristophanes' THE BIRDS, in a new adaptation by John Bellucci. The production, the third of the season, is being staged by resident director Elizabeth Duncan, and begins previews December 12 at 8 p.m. at the Old Baptist Church, One Dupuis Lane, Lakeside. THE BIRDS will join the current repertory of Webster's THE WHITE DEVIL and Pirandello's HENRY IV, and will run through March 20.

The production will feature an original musical score by Shirley Lefkowitz, which will be directed by the composer. The new adaptation by John Bellucci preserves the poetic meter of the songs and choral passages, and attempts to revitalize the topical references in the prose dialogue passages.

In addition to the resident acting company, the soloists and chorus of the Renaissance Motet Society will perform the birds' choral passages.

Sets for the production are by Rose Murphy, who designed last season's production of Behan's THE QUARE FELLOW. The costumes are designed by Scott Silviano, and happenings in the world ("Marlon Brando, who is on screen at the Rialto this weekend, is mentioned in the play now being performed at the Community Theatre").

Bad news in press releases is more likely to be printed than good news. But though thefts, fires, and bats may make the late edition, they can also make the audience decide to stay home. If you can make something good about your theatre sound like an important event, do so.

Remember: a press release cannot be just a rehash of a review. You can slip in a quoted adjective here and there, but news is events, not opinions.

An intriguing press release, accompanied by a cover letter and followed by a phone call, may even entice a reporter to write a feature story about your theatre or a member of it. A feature story can make your theatre a celebrity for a day. When fleeting fame touches you, do not succumb to its glitter. Instead, be increasingly attentive to the quality of your productions. Do not expect another story the next day, although the publicist should come up with a periodic stream of angles for continued features.

Sample Press Release
(continued)

the lighting by principal resident designer Patricia Wood.

Sponsorship for THE BIRDS and for the current production of HENRY IV comes from the Rita Phillips Foundation, which will also support the company's regional tour in the spring.

Performances are scheduled Tuesdays through Sundays at 8 p.m., with Saturday and Sunday matinees at 2:30 p.m. Ticket prices range from $5.00 to $10.00, depending on the day of the week. For group rates and individual tickets, call the Woodmere Theatre Company box office at 027-1960.

Sample Public Service Announcement
(to be released on letterhead stationery)

Note: Both the long and the short announcements can be sent to either television or radio stations, but television stations will most likely use only the 15-second release.

Woodmere Theatre Company
One Dupuis Lane   Lakeside, N.Y. 92145   332-027-1960

JANUARY 21, 1983
PUBLIC SERVICE ANNOUNCEMENT TO RUN AS OFTEN AS POSSIBLE
FROM JANUARY 25th THROUGH FEBRUARY 14th.

15 Seconds:

    THE WOODMERE THEATRE COMPANY OFFERS A FREE-LECTURE DEMONSTRATION ON SIGHT-SINGING, SUNDAY, FEBRUARY 14 AT 3 P.M., IN CONJUNCTION WITH ITS PRODUCTION OF A NEW ADAPTATION OF ARISTOPHANES' THE BIRDS, NOW IN REPERTORY WITH PIRANDELLO'S HENRY IV AND WEBSTER'S THE WHITE DEVIL. FOR INFORMATION CALL 027-1960, OR STOP BY THE BOX OFFICE AT THE WOODMERE THEATRE, ONE DUPUIS LANE. THE PHONE NUMBER AGAIN: 027-1960.

30 Seconds:

    THE WOODMERE THEATRE COMPANY IS OFFERING A FREE LECTURE-DEMONSTRATION ON SIGHT-SINGING ON SUNDAY, FEBRUARY 14th AT 3 P.M. THE WORKSHOP WILL TAKE PLACE IN THE OLD BAPTIST CHURCH, AND WILL BE LED BY CHARLES VLUDT, SOLOIST FROM THE RENAISSANCE MOTET SOCIETY, WHO WILL PERFORM IN THE WOODMERE THEATRE'S UPCOMING PRODUCTION OF ARISTOPHANES' THE BIRDS. FOR FURTHER INFORMATION ABOUT THIS WORKSHOP, OR THE BIRDS, OR ANY OF THE PRODUCTIONS NOW IN REPERTORY, CALL 027-1960, OR STOP BY THE WOODMERE THEATRE BOX OFFICE AT ONE DUPUIS LANE. THE PHONE NUMBER AGAIN IS 027-1960.

Public Service Announcements. In order to qualify for a public service announcement (or P.S.A.) of your production on radio or television, you must also be offering something to the public as a donation. This could be a reduced price or free tickets to senior citizens or the disabled, for example, or a special free performance given at the children's hospital. You can then mention that the play will continue its run at regular prices, and state the four essentials: what, where, when, and phone. There is no charge for such public service announcements, and they can be valuable publicity.

Check with the person in charge of public service announcements at each local station, to find out the proper length and format for your announcement. Often a television station will flash a slide on the screen as the announcement is made. You may provide a cogent photo for the visual, and you would be wise to impose your telephone number on it.

Recordings of scenes from the play on the air, whether videotaped or sound tape recorded, usually do not come off well at all. Acting values can seem wrenched out of proportion and the dialogue weirdly out of context, when what was intended for live theatre arrives over technologically manipulated airwaves. Let the audience learn about your production from as many sources as possible; but let them discover the play itself in your theatre.

Newsletters. The newsletter is a self-serving bulletin of information about your current, coming, and past seasons, which you send to your subscribers and to other organizations you wish to interest in your work. You are fooling no one that the newsletter is really news. But you can make it important: to set a literary example, as your production sets a theatrical one; or as a platform for philosophical and political musings, historical investigations, social searchings. Unfortunately it is rare that the newsletter is used in this way. Like every other mailing, the newsletter will involve the time and effort of everyone in the theatre. Make sure it contains something that is worth that energy.

Letters to the Editor. You may be tempted to write, or to have a friend write, a letter to the editor of a newspaper after an unfavorable review appears. Everyone will see through that ploy.

Even if a real stranger pens an irate rebuttal to the review, sadly, most readers will think it originated with you. It is very rare for real controversy between the critic and the public to stir up enough interest to increase attendance at your shows. Don't try to transform a hard-line review into a battle line. Take the bitter with the better, and stay committed to your task, which is to convince the audience of the merits of your art, not through argument, but through the art itself.

THE SUBSCRIPTION CAMPAIGN

Mounting a subscription campaign is a substantial investment of your money and your time. But with subscribers to your entire theatre season you will gain some guaranteed income and some guaranteed filled seats. To depend solely on individual ticket sales is to delight in teetering on the brink of nonexistence.

Weigh the benefits of a preordained schedule against the benefits of spontaneity. Naturally, you will say "subject to change" on your brochure; but if you change everything, your subscribers are likely to change their own minds about subscribing the next year. And there is a psychological advantage to promising a season ahead of time: you are more eager to keep your public promise than if you had merely whispered your intentions to your own image in the mirror.

It is unlikely that you will be able to make your theatre financially viable on the basis of subscribers, at least early in your history. But if your subscription campaign succeeds, you may want to contact the Foundation for the Extension and Development of the American Professional Theatre (FEDAPT) and move on to becoming, eventually, a not-so-small theatre. In any case, the bible of any subscription campaign is Danny Newman's book *Subscribe Now!* (Theatre Communications Group, 1977); to say more about the subject here would risk plagiarism or redundancy. Buy the book now!, as Danny Newman would say, and plan at least six months ahead of time for your subscription campaign.

Remember: a one percent return rate on a general mailing is considered average. If your mailing is targeted to the subscribers of similar institutions—symphonies, museums, other theatres— you can expect up to 10 percent return. If you are mailing a subscription offer to previous subscribers of your own theatre, you should realistically expect a more than 50 percent return rate. If your return rate is very much lower, consider rethinking what you are presenting on the stage.

In any mailing campaign there will be a few shortcuts. Go to the post office and acquire a nonprofit organization mailing permit before the piece is printed, so that your mailing indicia can be printed directly onto it. The post office will instruct you on how to bundle your mailing and label it according to zip codes. Try to make the folding, stuffing, and sealing of mailings as efficient as possible. You will need the aid of almost the entire company for each major mailing. Do not beg or whine; mailing campaigns are a recurrent necessity.

If you have the funds, you may want to look into a mailing service, especially if you are in a large urban area and there are lists available that are targeted to interest or geographical area. It is more logical to target subscribers than it is to try to target single ticket buyers. If you seek lists from other arts or service organizations, they may supply them at little or no fee; but you will eventually have to share yours with them as well.

One warning about all mailings: *Do not staple.* As the addressee rips open the stapled mailing, the message inside will invariably rip as well. Most mailings are filed quickly in the recipient's wastebasket; and the torn one will find its way there with even more alacrity.

There is some talk about a "subscription audience" being somehow less involved in the play they are viewing than a single ticket buyer might be. True, the single ticket buyer has decided recently to see this particular play. The subscriber made the decision to come long before, and it can be argued that he is more obligated than interested when the time of performance arrives. I question this logic. But even if it is true, it is up to the production to captivate the audience. There are as many reasons to blame an audience for your lack of magnetism as there are members of the audience. It is to no one's benefit, least of all the theatre's, to decry the playgoers.

Art, of course, is not measured by its popularity, nor by its lack of popular appeal. And pandering is an offense to honest standards. The artist must look to his own work to know its value. That is no doubt where the audience has been looking also.

12 Critics

THE MOST IMPORTANT CRITIC for any small theatre is the person who works in your theatre, but not directly on the production in progress; who has a keen eye for fuzziness and a keen ear for dissonance; who is unwilling to stand for either; and who is determined to stand up to say so. She should come to watch rehearsals about a week before the show is scheduled to open. These are the moments when she is the theatre's best friend. No excuses the director and the actors can think up will explain away the inadequacies she will find in your production. She has no reason to criticize, save that the show is not quite right yet. The theatre's best interests are her best interests. Listen, if you are the director. Speak up, if you are the critic.

This in-house critic may be the general manager, the house manager, the booking manager. The title matters not at all; all that she needs is perception and impatience. Consider yourself lucky indeed to have such a critic in your bosom. She may not know how to correct a defect; that is the job of the director. But she will know when something needs correcting, and her impetus can spur you on beyond complacency.

Be scrupulous, however, in allowing this vital spectator to

speak only to the director of the play, not to the actors or to the technical staff. Let the director translate for the company and crew, following his own instincts with regard to when, how much, and in what manner to instruct the company. Opening night may be soon, and the necessary changes may· be arduous and fragile.

Drastic last-minute alterations in scenes are called for more often than most theatre companies would like to admit. It is often not until a week before opening that one can run the show all the way through; and the effect of the whole may be quite different from what one had expected from responding to only bits and pieces. Sometimes, when something seems terribly wrong a very small change can make a very real improvement. Remember: it is not a condemnation of your entire being that a particular scene does not "work." It hurts to have your friend and manager keep saying "no good" to you. But it will hurt considerably more if you do not do something about it.

Aside from the in-house critic, there are two nomenclatures for critics: the *critic* and the *reviewer*. The former is the term used for the more literate opinionizer and interpreter; the latter is used for those who must grind out opinions on a tighter schedule.

The reviewer appears on the television or is heard on the radio, summing up the play and its quality in puns hurriedly scribbled in a taxicab speeding from the theatre to the station. These airborne reviews have the power to draw an audience to or away from your play with frightening magnetism.

The newspaper critic, sometimes considered to be a reviewer, usually has some Damoclean deadline to meet for his publication as well. But he at least has the opportunity to sit in front of a typewriter, to flip through research material, to think about sentence structure. Some critics—those who appear in magazines, journals, and books—will be responsible for the detailing of the life of a stage for generations of audiences who succeed the actual years of that stage. These writers influence few ticket sales. They make reputations.

Critics are a problem when they say something bad. Critics are also a problem when they say something good: it is not good enough; it is praise for the wrong reason. Remember, though, that if you believe the good words, you must believe the bad words also. It is better not to rely on outside approval for the estimation of your own value. Discover the strength of your own vision, and you will discover the strength of your own backbone.

According to ethical theatrical convention, you must invite critics to every production for which you are charging money. You will be able to think of thousands of reasons for wanting to keep those verbal wolves from your doors. If you insist on following through in your avoidance of critical acclaim or disdain, you have these options:

1. *Call the show a preview.* This labeling will work for a while. But the show really must be a preview: a few public performances being rehearsed or audience-tested at *reduced ticket prices.* During the period of preview, actors, technicians, and director must all be available for adjusting the show. Do not keep the show in preview for too long. Critics will get angry. Audiences will get edgy. Actors will lose the impulse to commit themselves to any decision at all. Be brave. Open the show.

2. *Call the show a "work in progress."* Beware. This phrase has become a catch-all for a hundred "experimental" theatres that take a year to "explore" a simplistic idea in a round robin of pretentious symbols, usually with a bowl of water and a bare breast. On rare and wonderful occasions, however, a "work in progress" can be an archaeological excavation through time, the theatre, and the soul. (I think of Meyerhold, dreaming of Hamlet waiting on the rocky coast for his wet and shivering father, ghostly, to walk from the cold sea. Hamlet removes his great cape from his shoulders and wraps it tenderly around the old man in his restless death; and father and son embrace in wind and shadow the time they did not know. Meyerhold never had the chance to stage his production.)

The label "work in progress" often invites a dangerous arrogance in the company that uses it. "My process is as important to you as my result, or even more so," it implies. Process is important. But process is a daily effort of hours together, with sweat, unguarded tongues, hope, connivance, ritual, spontaneous improvisation; many, many failures for every consummated moment on the stage. Is presenting a half-finished play really treating the audience to a "work in progress"? Would you willingly invite an audience to watch a full day of rehearsal? Be honest with yourself, and you will become more capable of dealing with the attention and the reflections, however distorted, of public critics.

3. *Offer free performances.* If you are not asking for money, you have the right to ask for no reviews. In this case the critic cannot justly claim that he must protect the public from the misspending of their money. Unfortunately, sometimes the production that costs nothing is in fact worthless. At other times, though, it is a priceless gift; but because there are not critics present, few will hear of it at all.

4. *Do extraordinarily bad productions.* If you keep this up for several years, the critics will probably have given up on you anyway.

Theatres need critics, despite the months of effort they spend thinking up ugly epithets and obsequious welcomes for them. Your main difficulty will be not in keeping them away, but in getting them to come at all.

Send each critic—for newspapers, magazines, radio, and television—an invitation to the opening or the "press opening" performance, which is usually the first regular public performance after two or three previews. Follow up with a telephone call within the week; but do not call the critic at home unless he has specifically requested that you do so. Offer him a pair of free tickets. Ask if there is any particular location he prefers, such as the aisle, the front row, near an exit; or if he has any special needs, such as a parking space or a quick cab after the show.

Every critic should receive a "press kit" when he arrives at the box office for the show. This packet contains two black-and-white glossy photographs of a scene from the show, appropriately backed with the names of the players and their roles; information telling when, where, and for how long the show will be playing; a program; and possibly some nonjudgmental information about the play or your theatre. You can also include a ball-point pen and a small flashlight. It is bad form to include copies of other reviews in the press kit. After the show has been in production for a time and the reviewers have had an opportunity to comment on it, you can make copies of particularly good reviews and place them discreetly around your lobby or on your walls.

Do not quote in your advertisements the one good sentence

in a bad review. This is deceptive, and rightfully irks the critic so used.

After the review appears, do not thank the critic for a good review unless you are equally prepared to thank him for a poor one. You do your job, and he does his. And do not acknowledge to the reviewer that anything bad he has said is true. Such affirmation will only encourage him to search for more bad things in future productions, as a measure of both his wisdom and his new duty. You may speak well of the critic's writing style, however. That is a separate art, and can be considered free from your theatre's influence on it.

You may thank a critic if he notices something very special, very small, and has liked it. This lets the critic know that you are grateful for the careful attention he has paid to detail, and therefore the respect he has given to your work.

The theatre may find the critic to be blindfolded, earmuffed, lacking in taste, or self-serving—not to mention bitter or jealous, if he has aspired to theatre in his past. But be thankful for him. His aid can bring in an audience. His notices may help you gain future grant monies. He keeps your reputation alive even when the theatre itself is dark. And if all else fails, be thankful you are not a critic yourself.

The critic is your partner in the service of the theatre, however thorny a marriage it may seem to be. He regards himself as an avenue between the performance and the public; and he considers that avenue, in language as well as perception, to be an art in itself. He wishes to inform the audience in graceful prose of what they may discover if they attend the performance, and also of what is there that they might not see without his guidance. The poor notice the critic gave you could have been caused by the stale fish he ate for dinner, but it could equally have been the result of his own passion for the nourishment of theatre, and his real need to serve its audience.

13 Tours, Bookings, and Groups

THERE ARE THREE TYPES OF SALES other than single tickets and subscriptions: group sales, bookings, and tours. In this discussion a *group* is a number of persons (determined by the theatre, but usually ten or more) who attend a performance together after making a previous reservation for tickets at a reduced rate; a *booking* is a performance not scheduled as part of a regular run of a play, which has been requested, and prepaid for, by some organization; a *tour* is any performance outside your own theatre. Other lexicons use the terms booking and tour interchangeably, but the procedure of setting up and carrying through an extra performance anywhere is complicated enough to merit a titular distinction.

The organizations most likely to form groups that will invite you to visit them or come to visit you are colleges and universities, social clubs such as the Y.M.C.A., Great Books Clubs, and various charities seeking fundraising events. These last will buy tickets from you at the price you ask, and then resell them at a higher rate, keeping the difference as a donation to their services.

If another theatre expresses interest in an exchange of visits, expect the profit to be in ideas and theatrical invention, not in money.

If you wait for an invitation, it probably will not come. Occasionally professors from universities will come to your theatre, see a play, and say, "I'd love to bring you to our school." It is up to a member of your theatre to follow up on such casual remarks. Seeking out tours, bookings, and group sales can be a full-time job for a member of your administrative staff. I recommend that the person who serves as booking manager be paid within the guidelines of the point system described in chapter 2 rather than on commission. Her salary should reflect her position as a member of your theatre.

The booking manager will probably have responsibility for group sales as well. This confluence of jobs is logical, not only for the salary involved but also because there is so much calendar coordination necessary in getting a theatre company together. Remember: most of the actors and technical staff will probably have to supplement their incomes by working outside the small theatre. They will have to juggle their own schedules to be available for any extra performances.

There are independent booking agencies that set up tours for lecturers and certain artistic companies. There are also individual entrepreneurs who will offer you their booking services for a fee. Booking agencies, however, do try to limit themselves to theatres that are already known. And the independent entrepreneur may be more interested in establishing his own identity than that of your theatre. You will have to monitor very carefully every piece of information that he sends out concerning your company. This procedure can be just as much work as having an in-house booking manager, and a lot more worry. Also, when a sudden and unexpected change of plan occurs, as it often does in small theatre, it is better for a member of your own theatre to be able to telephone with a gracious explanation than to have it appear in bureaucratese from the hand of a third party.

One of the most useful aspects of both the booking agency and the individual entrepreneur, though, is that they will supply charts showing how much various organizations have paid for performances by other companies. (They will often give you these charts to encourage you to use their services, as proof of how much they can make for you.) The range is enormous—from $300 for an hour-long children's theatre matinee to $10,000 for a week's residence at a large university. If your booking manager can possibly get some idea of what the sponsor is willing to pay before stating your fee, you can avoid some embarrassing bargaining blunders.

The most useful tools for the booking manager are the yellow pages for your immediate area and Barron's guide to colleges and universities, which lists schools across the country. Send a letter and a flier to every business and school that could possibly be interested, and say why your specific play will appeal to this particular organization. Enclose a return card on which they can note their interest, and follow up every reply with a telephone call. Pursue even some of those who do not return the card. Keep in mind that you truly have something remarkable, meritorious, even unique to offer these places of business and learning. If you do not tell them about your good work they may not hear of it, and thus will miss the opportunity, and the pleasure, of viewing it.

The small theatre is free, within limits, to set different prices for performing the same play to different organizations. You have a right to charge more to the wealthier groups, especially on a traveling tour. Funding from one engagement may be sufficient to cover the cost of all traveling expenses, enabling you to travel "free" to other institutions along the way. One organization may hear from another about the difference in cost. If you have justified it in your own mind, you will be able fearlessly to justify it in theirs. Remember also, when budgeting for tours and bookings, to figure in the extra costs incurred by traveling and eating on the road while at the same time you are paying rent and utilities at your resident theatre space.

The patience of the booking manager must be continually replenished. There will be so many more no's than yes's. But the number of tickets at any one yes can be substantial. The money from tours and bookings will often mean the difference between red and black in the small theatre ledger. Spectators from a group sale will often crowd an otherwise empty house. Be persistent. It is the audience that completes the event of theatre.

TOURS

Going on tour with a theatre company is the equivalent of taking a long walk with twelve little puppies who have diarrhea. There are two types of tours: those that permit the company to return home the same day, and those farther away, involving overnight stays. To arrange and organize props, vehicles, gasoline, pickup of actors, striking and rebuilding a set, and quickly getting comfortable on a new stage is a monstrous task. Therefore all of those short tours, which allow you to return the same day, would be better arranged as bookings at your theatre.

Tours involving overnight stays, on the other hand, are the most lucrative short-term work of the small theatre. Be happy when the contract for a tour comes through, and prepare for as many eventualities as you can. On tour, even more than in your own theatre, everything that can go wrong will—a maxim that is even more prone to proof in strange cities and isolated universities than in your own home town. Make lists of what to take, and double check them.

A minimum of three persons outside the cast should come on all overnight tours:

• One to be in charge of everything technical that needs to be done on the stage—including having a crew available from the organization to which you are traveling. This is generally the stage manager.

• One to be in charge of all lodging, eating, and toilet arrangements; the maintenance of the van in which you travel; and the scheduling of drivers from within the company who are confident about driving the van and who will not become over-tired by driving. This is often the booking manager, who has already had contact with the organization by mail or telephone.

• One, usually the director, who oversees everything. She lends a hand at each turn, especially in rehearsing on the new stage. Acoustical tests will be necessary, and some blocking changes. On the evening of the performance, she can lend a hand with house-managerial duties.

It is helpful if one of these three is a registered nurse, or at least has some general first-aid experience. All dancers have muscle sprains, and all singers have laryngitis. It is a good idea if one of

The Importance of Lists

"WHAT'S the matter, Asher? You're so late getting up this morning to feed your chickens!"

"Well, Moishe, when I go to bed at night, I take my clothes off."

"Good."

"But when I get up in the morning, I can't remember where I put them. It takes me so long to get dressed that I'm late feeding my chickens."

"Oh, that's easy. Take a pencil and a paper and make a *list*. When you get undressed write down where you put your shoes, where you put your shirt, where you put your pants, where you put your hat. Then, when you get up in the morning, you'll read where everything is."

"Oh, thank you, Moishe! I can't wait to go to sleep tonight!"

That evening Asher wrote as he got undressed: "My shoes are on the floor. My shirt is on the chandelier. My pants are over the doorknob. My hat is on the windowsill. Oh!," wrote Asher as he pulled the covers up to his chin, "and I am in bed."

"Mmmm," said Asher. "I can't wait to get up in the morning." And he fell asleep.

At dawn Asher awoke with the rooster's crow, reached for his list, and began, smiling, to dress himself. " 'My shoes are on the floor,'" he read. And so they were. "This is remarkable!" thought Asher. " 'My shirt is on the chandelier.'" And so it was. " 'My pants are over the doorknob'—yes! And my hat is on the windowsill! All dressed—and ready to feed my chicke—— Just a minute! There's one more thing on my list. 'And I am in bed.' "

Asher looked. "But I am not there!" he said. "Where am I? What good is finding all my clothes if I myself am lost?"

these three is a licensed mechanic. All vans have overheated radiators; the locks on all trunks jam. An occasional psycho-therapeutic session may also find its way onto the lonely roads of the tour.

The company will generally be bedded in dormitory rooms at a college, or in the homes of officers of the organization sponsoring your tour. Request that lodging be as close to the theatre as possible—walking distance is almost essential—and that as many members of the company as possible be housed together. Be sure that there are beverages and bathrooms available at the theatre the whole time the company is setting up, rehearsing, performing, or teaching workshops. Have at hand the phone number and an alternate number for someone at the sponsoring organization who will come to your aid should the probable crisis develop.

A tour usually consists of stops at more than one college or organization. When planning a tour, the booking manager should have a map handy, and try to plan the itinerary so that you are not alternating travel in different directions. Allow, if possible, time for one long nap before each performance in a new location. You will often want to strike your set and hightail it out of town immediately after the performance. This is a good idea. Better to arrive early in the new town, have some time to walk around the theatre, test the acoustics and the floorboards, learn how to operate the lightboards, give the new ushers their assignments, say to your host "Sorry I can't spend more time with you"—and still have time for that nap before the performance.

There is no way that you will be able to rehearse a new show while you are on tour with another. There are too many adjustments to make to new spaces. In addition, you may have to shorten your play, add intermissions, censor dialogue, and devise workshops to give after performances.

You will have little time to be a tourist. Bring a camera anyway. There will be moments to remember. Do not tell yourself that you are bringing culture to the boondocks. These strangers are your audience; and your audience is your equal.

Be sure that you have left your children with a competent babysitter and your theatre with a working answering machine or service. There are so many things to think about—and yes, babysitter and your theatre with a working answering machine or service. There are so many things to think about—and yes, even to enjoy—on tour that it is a shame if your mind is continually on an unfinished problem back home.

The camaraderie of a tour can prove short-lived, and is therefore often misapprehended as false. But it is real while it lasts, and its comfort provides compensatory security for the unpredictability of performances on strange stages before alien audiences.

Just as the space in which you are working will be different from the one to which you are accustomed, so the reaction from your audience can differ markedly from what you have been used to at home. For this reason the play that you take on tour must be very well rehearsed, and the actors must have experience in performing it as well—not so that it may be the same, but so they might handle comfortably and in character the caprices of geographical variety. Your audience on tour may laugh in the place you least expect; or applaud; or not applaud; or walk out. Do not pander; do not put them down. Stay true to the essence of your production, while making every effort to discover the most exciting means of communication to these people you may meet just once in a theatrical lifetime. The art of theatre is not the art of compromise. But if you can make a change that clarifies a performance for an audience, or facilitates their acceptance of the essence of your production, then you may not have compromised at all, but rather stumbled upon a new avenue between the spirits of men. Even censorship, from time to time, can be opportune, when you realize that you must develop a look, a movement, instead of the easy utterance of the offensive word.

The tour is often worth the trouble: for its financial benefits, which can be considerable; for the invigoration of a change in atmosphere and the challenge of awkward or elegant new spaces in which to work; and for the reassurance that, while your work may not be universal, at least it has appeal from Islip to Iowa.

BOOKINGS

Logistically it is clearly far easier for you to bring an audience to your theatre than it is for you to go out on tour. The audience is only people. You are people, things, and a home space. If the sponsoring organization is within a comfortable day's journey, suggest to them that they find transportation and come to you.

The price you set for this arrangement will be less than the price you would charge to go to them, which should encourage their willingness to travel. It is true that your profit decreases, but the strain on your company is so much lessened that it is truly worth considering. But if you sell the entire house for a special performance during the day or on some night you would not otherwise perform, you can ethically charge more than you would for each seat sold at a regular performance. You are legitimately spending extra time preparing this performance, and neglecting other rehearsals or commitments. This special effort merits special compensation.

GROUPS

It is also possible, and a major part of the booking manager's job, to arrange *group sales*, which are blocks of a certain number of tickets sold at a discount to an organization or group for a regular performance. Birthday parties, retirement celebrations, anniversary commemoratives, office parties can all be occasions for a group outing to the theatre. The more of these invented occasions a booking manager can think up and give title to, plus the more organizations she can telephone and follow up by mail, the more successful your ticket sales will be. It is extremely unwise to depend on single ticket sales to supply a house. Every theatre, small and large, needs groups.

Discounts are usually given on a sliding scale, depending on the number in the group in proportion to the size of your theatre. Today's discount will bring in additional revenue tomorrow; some in the group that watches your play tonight will tell friends about the performance, and individual ticket sales will increase next week.

CODA

Try not to ponder with too much melancholy the question, "Why are they willing to pay $3,000 for me to perform this play in Utah, when they complain about the price of a three-dollar ticket at home?" Who needs to be a hero, anyway, even in his own country?

14 Conclusion

ACTORS WILL LEAVE A THEATRE for many reasons, not just money, tiffs, roles, television, directors. An actor needs a thousand lives. Let him take them. You who remain in the theatre without him will be jealous, hurt, angry, empty. Try not to act on those feelings, although they never fully fade.

Like the actor, others will leave. Leavetakings are as natural as sunset. The theatre's space may be taken from you. The debts of the theatre may become excessive. Your will may shift to other purposes. Almost every small theatre dies, eventually; the average life span of a small theatre that survives for more than one season is six seasons.

There are so many reasons for the final locking of the theatre's doors, the cardboard boxing of mailing lists, the returning to Goodwill of costumes, the sale of lights and tools and typewriters. All the reasons bear some burden of the sad, inevitable truth. Try not to dwell on any of them, or to identify the most substantial one. Try not to live again and again through that final moment. The vital moments in the theatre are in that theatre's life. The miracle is that a small theatre can live for any time at all, and that its magic can bind us forever.

Appendix: Where to Study, What to Read

THE BEST TRAINING for anyone who wishes to work in theatre is in a good theatre. The example of those you admire and the opportunity for you to try are the preceptors of choice for any artist.

Some specific skills of the technician and craftsman—use of tools, properties of materials, for example—can be easily introduced in designated courses. The administrator can benefit from familiarity with tested accounting methods. But for both the technician and the administrator practice makes these skills more naturally available.

It is important that designers be intimate with the histories of the arts of many cultures. The actor will profit from instruction with a qualified teacher in certain skills such as juggling and tumbling. Actor and director both can gain much from the guided study of a variety of literary traditions, as well as of anthropology, sociology, and psychology.

"Acting," "directing," "design" can be experimented with in schools, but their elevation is better served by the relentless process of unapologetic self-evaluation and the evaluation of those you trust. Schools can be of great help in giving you a chance to meet people who may offer you future work. But you can also brush against persons there who for some infraction or irreverence on your part will swear never to hire you as long as either of you works.

Beware especially continual "workshops," which tend to perpetuate themselves and their leaders rather than encourage the creation of an event to be shared with an audience. A cult is not an art, and the artist must be the master of his own expressive spirit.

There are many, many books, periodicals, and service organizations for information in all aspects of theatre. I have selected a few I find valuable for this appendix. But remember: the knowledge is in the doing; the doing is not in the knowledge.

Sweat, tears, smiles, and the unwillingness to cease until an explosion of yes threatens to break your heart: therein is the fulfillment of theatre.

I. Bibliography

This is a selective listing of books related to each of the chapters in this handbook. They are arranged by chapter, according to their relevance to the subject at hand. Naturally, some chapters overlap in their general outlines, and so for a complete reference list on finance, for example, it is best to consult "Administration and Budget," "Publicity," and "Raising Money."

Bibliographical works and general works on theatre have been placed under chapter 1, "Choosing to Be."

The prices given after each entry are those of mid-1981 and are, of course, subject to change.

For more comprehensive listings, consult *Performing Arts Books in Print*, and its supplements, as listed below.

CHAPTER 1: Choosing to Be

Adelman, Irving, and Dworkin, Rita, compilers. *Modern Drama: A Checklist of Critical Literature on 20th Century Plays.* Metuchen, N.J.: Scarecrow Press, 1967. $10.00. A selective survey of the critical literature of 20th century drama.

Artaud, Antonin. *The Theatre and Its Double.* New York: Grove Press, 1958. $3.95.

Baker, Blanch M. *Theatre and Allied Arts.* New York: Blom, 1967. $17.50. A reference guide divided into three main parts: (1) drama, theatre, and actors; (2) stagecraft and allied arts; (3) miscellaneous reference material.

Bentley, Eric. *The Theatre of Commitment.* New York: Atheneum, 1967. $4.95.

Bentley, Eric. *What Is Theatre?* New York: Atheneum, 1968. $4.95.

Brustein, Robert. *The Culture Watch: Essays on Theatre and Society.* New York: Alfred A. Knopf, 1975. $7.95.

Brustein, Robert. *Making Scenes.* New York: Random House, 1981. $15.00. Brustein's views on the foundation, development, and displacement of his repertory theatre at Yale.

Brustein, Robert. *The Theatre of Revolt.* Boston: Little, Brown, 1964. $6.95.

Bryant, Donald C.; Brockett, Oscar C.; and Becker, Samuel L. *A Bibliographical Guide to Research in Speech and Dramatic Art.* New York: Scott, Foresman, 1963. $3.50.

Kott, Jan. *The Eating of the Gods.* New York: Random House, 1973. $8.50.

Kott, Jan. *Shakespeare, Our Contemporary.* London: Methuen, 1964. $4.95.

Lane, Marc J. *Legal Handbook for Non-Profit Organizations.* New York: Amacom, 1980. $17.95.

Performing Arts Books in Print. New York: Drama Book Specialists, 1973, with yearly supplements.

CHAPTER 2: Administration and Budget

Foundation for the Extension and Development of the American Professional Theatre. *Box Office Guidelines.* New York: FEDAPT, 1977. $7.50.

Hanlon, R. Brendan. *A Guide to Taxes and Record-Keeping for Performers, Designers, and Directors.* New York: Drama Book Specialists, 1980. $4.95, tax-deductible.

Langley, Stephen. *Producers on Producing.* New York: Drama Book Specialists, 1976. $8.95.

Langley, Stephen. *Theatre Management in America.* New York: Drama Book Specialists, 1980. $7.95.

CHAPTER 3: Raising Money

Foundation for the Extension and Development of the American Professional Theatre. *Subscription Guidelines.* New York: FEDAPT, 1977. $7.50.

The Foundation Directory. New York: The Foundation Center, published annually. (Distributed by Columbia Press.) A *Directory of Foundations* for each individual state is also available from the Division of Public Charities, care of the state attorney general's office.

Pendleton, Neil. *Fund-Raising: A Guide to Non-Profit Organization.* Englewood, N.J.: Prentice-Hall Spectrum Books, 1981. $6.95.

Social Register. New York: SRA, published annually. $35.00.

CHAPTER 4: Space

Arnheim, Rudolf. *Visual Thinking.* Davis: University of California Press, 1969. $11.50. Although not a "theatre book," *Visual Thinking* describes problem solving in the arts, within the context of a general discussion of fundamental processes of vision and perception.

Corry, Percy. *Planning the Stage.* London: Pitman Publishing Co., 1961. $7.95.

Elder, Eldon. *Will It Make a Theatre?* New York: Drama Book Specialists, 1979. $6.95.

Stephen, Joseph. *New Theatre Forms.* New York: Theatre Arts Books, 1968. $6.25.

Thomas, Richard K. *Three-Dimensional Design: The Cellular Approach.* New York: Reinhold, 1969. $6.95. Again, not a "theatre book," but the discussion of cellular theory in relation to display, lighting, housing design, and planning should be of use to renovators and designers.

CHAPTER 5: Choosing the Play

Annotated Bibliography of New Publications in the Performing Arts. New York: Drama Book Shop, 1970, four times yearly. $2.50.

Cole, Toby, editor. *Playwrights on Playwriting.* New York: Hill and Wang, 1960. $3.95.

Kay, Phyllis Johnson. *National Playwrights Directory.* Waterford, Conn.: O'Neill Theatre Center Project, 1977. $10.00. This valuable volume includes the names and synopses of 400 published and unpublished plays by living American playwrights.

Samples, Gordon. *The Drama Scholar's Index to Plays and Film-scripts.* Metuchen, N.J.: Scarecrow Press, 1974. Vol. 1: $12.50; Vol. 2: $30.00.

CHAPTER 6: Director

Braun, Edward. *Meyerhold on Theatre.* New York: Hill and Wang, 1969. $8.50. This collection of writings covers Meyerhold's entire career as a director from 1902 to 1939. The critical commentary relates Meyerhold and his work to his historical period, and describes his major productions. The book includes 50 photographs of Meyerhold's designs and productions.

Brook, Peter. *The Empty Space.* New York: Atheneum, 1980. $3.95. An explanation and discussion of the theories and techniques involved in Brook's productions of *King Lear, The Visit, Marat/Sade,* and others.

Cole, Toby, and Chinoy, Helen Krich. *Directors on Directing.* New York: Bobbs-Merrill, 1963. $4.25.

Gielgud, John. *Stage Directions.* New York: Random House, 1963. $5.95.

Gorchakov, Nicolai. *Stanislavski Directs.* New York: Funk & Wagnall, 1954. $4.95. Diaries and notes from rehearsals, 1924–1936.

Grotowski, Jerzy. *Towards a Poor Theatre.* New York: Simon and Schuster, 1969. $6.50, cloth; $2.45, paper. Texts by, and interviews with, the Polish director-producer, with supplementary material presenting his method and training.

Johnson, Albert, and Johnson, Bertha. *Directing Methods.* New York: A. S. Barnes, 1970. $9.50. This book treats dramatic analysis, theatrical styles, dynamics of movement, theatre technology, and management and promotion as they have evolved from Meininger to contemporary directors.

Roose-Evans, James. *Directing a Play*. New York: Theatre Arts Books, 1968. $6.95. An attempt to detail the job of the director from the first reading to the opening night and after.

Simonov, Ruben. *Stanislavski's Protege: Eugene Vakhtangov*. New York: Drama Book Specialists, 1969. $6.95. A detailed account of rehearsals of Chekhov's *A Wedding* is followed by a critical comparison of Vakhtangov's and Stanislavski's treatments of Chekhov. In describing the evolution of Soviet theatre, Simonov uncovers interesting accounts of attempts by Maeterlinck, Meyerhold, and Vakhtangov to work together.

Tairov, Alexander. *Notes of a Director*. Miami: University of Miami Press, 1969. $6.50. A record of the first six years of the Moscow Kamerny Theatre and the theories that stimulated its foundation.

CHAPTER 7: Actor

Chaikin, Joseph. *The Presence of the Actor*. New York: Atheneum, 1977. $3.95. Notes on the Open Theatre, disguises, acting, and repression.

Chekhov, Michael. *To the Actor: On the Technique of Acting*. New York: Harper and Row, 1953. $6.00.

Cole, Toby, and Chinoy, Helen Krich, editors. *Actors on Acting*. New York: Crown, 1970. $8.95.

Dunn, Charles J., and Torigoe, Bunzo. *The Actors' Analects*. New York: Columbia Press, 1969. $11.00. This unusual book prints for the first time in English the extant writings by the great Japanese actors of the popular theatre of the late 17th century.

Fast, Julius. *Body Language*. New York: Lippincott, 1970. $4.95. Although this is not a "theatre book," it discusses the science of kinetics, and the relationship between gesture and the spoken word in the amplification or contradiction of intention.

Hobbs, William. *Stage Fight*. New York: Theatre Arts Books, 1967. $6.95.

Kierkegaard, Soren. *Crisis in the Life of an Actress, and Other Essays on Drama*. New York: Harper and Row, 1967. $1.45.

Lessac, Arthur. *Training of the Use of the Human Voice*. New York: Drama Book Specialists, 1967. $8.00.

Redgrave, Michael. *Mask or Face: Reflections in an Actor's Mirror*. New York: Theatre Arts Books, 1958. $4.15.

Stanislavski, Konstantin. *An Actor's Handbook*. New York: Theatre Arts Books, 1979. $3.95.

Stanislavski, Konstantin. *An Actor Prepares*. New York: Theatre Arts Books, 1979. $9.95.

Stanislavski, Konstantin. *Building a Character*. New York: Theatre Arts Books, 1979. $9.95.

Stanislavski, Konstantin. *Creating a Role*. New York: Theatre Arts Books, 1979. $9.95.

Stanislavski, Konstantin. *My Life in Art*. New York: Theatre Arts Books, 1979. $8.95.

CHAPTER 8: Rehearsal

Boleslavski, Richard. *Acting: The First Six Lessons*. New York: Theatre Arts Books, 1933. $3.25. Essays in dialogue form on concentration, emotion-memory, dramatic action, characterization, observation, and rhythm, by the director of the first studio of the Moscow Art Theatre.

Jones, Robert Edmond. *The Dramatic Imagination*. New York: Theatre Arts Books, 1941. $3.95.

Shaw, George Bernard. *The Art of Rehearsal*. New York: Samuel French, 1928. Though long out of print, this letter of advice from Shaw to an Irish colleague is available in libraries in pamphlet form and essay collections.

CHAPTER 9: Designer and Crew

Set Design and Construction:

Bablet, Denis. *Le Decor de Theatre*. Paris: Editions du Centre Nationale de la Recherche Scientifique, 1965. $22.00.

Basic Carpentry (Illustrated). Menlo Park, Calif.: Lane Publishing Co., 1980. $3.95.

Basic Wiring. Alexandria, Va.: Time-Life Books, 1978. $7.95.

Craig, Edward Gordon. *On the Art of the Theatre*. New York: Theatre Arts Books, 1958. $6.50.

Craig, Edward Gordon. *Scene*. New York: Blom (Arno Press), 1968. $12.50.

Craig, Edward Gordon. *Towards a New Theatre*. New York: Blom (Arno Press), 1969. $27.50.

Gillette, A. S. *An Introduction to Scene Design*. New York: Harper and Row, 1967. $15.95.

Gillette, A. S. *Stage Scenery: Its Construction and Rigging*. New York: Harper and Row, 1972. $28.35.

Graham, Frank D. *Carpenters' and Builders' Guide*. Indianapolis: Audel (Bobbs-Merrill), 1965. Four volumes, $18.00.

Jones, Robert Edmond. *Drawings for the Theatre*. New York: Theatre Arts Books, 1970. $13.50.

Joseph, Stephen. *Scene Painting and Design*. London: Pitman Publishing Co., 1964. $6.95.

Parker, W. Oren. *Sceno-Graphic Techniques*. Carnegie Institute, 1964. $5.75.

Costume Design:

Anthony, Pegaret, and Arnold, Janet. *Costume: A General Bibliography*. London: Costume Society of the Victoria and Albert Museum, 1966. $2.00.

Payne, Blanche. *History of Costume*. New York: Harper and Row, 1965. $28.50.

Russell, Douglas A. *Stage Costume Design, Theory, Technique, and Style*. Englewood Cliffs, N.J.: Prentice-Hall, 1973. $27.50.

Lighting Design:

Bentham, Frederick. *The Art of Stage Lighting*. New York: Theatre Arts Books, 1976. $19.95.

Gillette, J. Michael. *Designing with Light*. Palo Alto: Mayfield Publishing Co., 1978. $8.95.

Other:

Buchman, Herman. *Stage Makeup*. London: Pitman Publishing Co., 1972. $21.50.

Burris-Meyer, Harold; Mallory, Vincent; and Goodfriend, Lewis. *Sound in the Theatre*. New York: Theatre Arts Books, 1979. $14.95.

Gruver, Bert, and Hamilton, Frank. *The Stage Manager's Handbook*. New York: Drama Book Specialists, 1979. $7.95.

Keaton, Warren. *Stage Properties and How to Make Them*. New York: Drama Book Specialists, 1978. $6.95.

CHAPTER 11: Publicity

Kother, Philip. *Marketing for Non-Profit Organizations.* Engle-
    wood, N.J.: Prentice-Hall, 1975. $14.95. This guide is not
    specifically related to the theatre.
McArthur, Nancy. *How to Do Theatre Publicity.* Bevea, Ohio:
    Good Ideas Company, 1978. $19.50.
Newman, Danny. *Subscribe Now! Building an Audience Through
    Dynamic Subscription Promotion.* New York: Theatre
    Communications Group, 1977. $12.95, cloth; $7.95,
    paper.

CHAPTER 13: Tours, Bookings, and Groups

Barron's Profiles of American Colleges. Woodbury, N.Y.: Barron's
    Educational Series, Inc., published annually.

II. Theatre Journals and Periodicals

This is a selective listing of the many journals and periodicals
about theatre published in the United States and abroad. Publishers' addresses accompany each title.

UNITED STATES

Comparative Drama. Western Michigan University, Dept. of Eng-
    lish, Kalamazoo, Mich. 49008.
Contributions in Drama and Theatre Studies. Greenwood Press, 51
    Riverside Ave., Westport, Conn. 06880.
Drama Review. New York University, Room 300, School of the
    Arts, 51 West 4th St., New York, N.Y. 10012.
Modern International Drama. State University of New York, Max
    Reinhardt Archive, Binghamton, N.Y. 13901.
New York Theatre Critics' Reviews. Critics Theatre Reviews, Inc.,
    4 Park Ave., New York, N.Y. 10016.
Performing Arts Journal. Box 858, Peter Stuyvesant Station, New
    York, N.Y. 10009.
Performing Arts Review. Law Arts Publishers, Inc., 453 Greenwich
    St., New York, N.Y. 10013.
Praxis: A Journal of Radical Perspectives on the Arts. Box 1280,
    Santa Monica, Calif. 90416.

Shakespeare Quarterly. Folger Shakespeare Library, 201 East Capitol St., SE, Washington, D.C. 20003.

Shakespeare Survey. Cambridge University Press, 32 East 57th St., New York, N.Y. 10022.

Theatre. Yale Theatre, Box 2046, Yale Station, New Haven, Conn. 06520.

Theatre Crafts. Rodale Press, Inc., Organic Park, Emmaus, Penn. 18049.

Theater Journal. American Theatre Association, 1000 Vermont Ave., NW, Washington, D.C. 20005.

Theatre Survey. American Society for Theatre Research, University of Pittsburgh, 1117 Cathedral of Learning, Pittsburgh, Penn. 15260.

West Coast Plays. P.O. Box 7206, Berkeley, Calif. 94707.

ENGLAND

Drama. British Theatre Association, 9 Fitzroy Square, London W1P 6AE, England.

Theatre Notebook. Society for Theatre Research, 14 Woronzow Road, London NW8 6QE, England.

Theatre Quarterly. TQ Publications, Ltd., 44 Earlham St., London WC2H 9LA, England.

Theatre Research International. Oxford Press, Press Rd., Neasden, London NW10 ODD, England.

CANADA

Canadian Theatre Review. CTR Publications, York University, 200B Administrative Studies, 4700 Keele St., Downsview, Ontario, Canada M3J IP3.

Modern Drama. A. M. Hakkert Ltd., 554 Spadina Crescent, Toronto, Ontario, Canada M5S 2J9.

Performing Arts in Canada. Canadian Stage Arts Publications, Ltd., Box 517, Station F, Toronto, Ontario, Canada M44 IT4.

FRANCE

Avant Scene Theater. Editions Avant Scene, 27 Rue St. Andre des Arts, 75006, Paris, France.

ITALY

Theater Annual. John Cabot Intern College, Viale Pola 12, 00298, Rome, Italy.

GERMANY

Theater Heute. Erhard Friedrich Verlag, IM Brande 15, 3016 Seelze G., Federal Republic of Germany.

SHOW–BUSINESS PERIODICALS

Backstage. 152 East 74th St., New York, N.Y. 10021. Published weekly, 75 cents.

Variety. 154 West 46th St., New York, N.Y. 10036. Published weekly, $1.00.

Plays and Players. Hansom Books, P.O. Box 294, 2 & 4 Pye St., Westminster, London SW1P 2LR, England. 75 pence.

III. Publishers and Distributors

Associated Council of the Arts, 1564 Broadway, New York, N.Y. 10036.

Baker's Play Company, 100 Chauncey St., Boston, Mass. 02111.

Dodd Mead, 79 Madison Ave., New York, N.Y. 10016.

Drama Book Specialists, 150 West 52nd St., New York, N.Y. 10036.

Dramatists Play Service, 440 Park Ave. South, New York, N.Y. 10016.

Faber and Faber, 3 Queen Square, London WC1, England.

Frederick Ungar Publishing Co., 250 Park Ave. South, New York, N.Y. 10003.

Grove Press (Evergreen–Black Cat Editions), 53 East 11th St., New York, N.Y. 10003.

Methuen and Co., Ltd., 11 New Fetter Lane, EC4 London, England.

The New American Library (Signet, Signet Classics, Mentor, Plume, Meridian, and NAL Editions), 1633 Broadway, New York, N.Y. 10019.

Penguin Books, 625 Madison Ave., New York, N.Y. 10022.
S. G. Phillips, Inc., 305 West 86th St., New York, N.Y. 10024.
Samuel French, Inc., 25 West 45th St., New York, N.Y. 10036.
Theatre Arts Books, 333 6th Ave., New York, N.Y. 10014.
University of Chicago Press, Chicago, Ill. 60637.
University Press of Hawaii, 2840 Kolowalu St., Honolulu, Hawaii
    96822.
Wadsworth Publishing Co., 10 Davis Drive, Belmont, Calif.
    94002.

IV. Catalogues

For examples of catalogues of lighting equipment, write to:

Aladdin Stage Lighting, Inc., 510 South St., Philadelphia, Penn.
    19147.
Stage Lighting Rental Service, 170 Gilbert Ave., New Haven,
    Conn. 06511.

For makeup catalogues, write to:

The Makeup Center, Inc., 80 Boylston St., Boston, Mass. 02116.

V. Major Shakespeare Festivals in the U.S.
(under LORT contracts)

American Shakespeare Theatre, 1850 Elm St., Stratford, Conn.
    06497.
Champlain Shakespeare Festival, Royall Tyler Theatre, Univer-
    sity of Vermont, Burlington, Vt. 05401.
Great Lakes Shakespeare Festival, Lakewood Civic Auditorium,
    Franklin Boulevard and Bunts Road, Lakewood, Ohio
    44107.
L.A. Free Shakespeare Festival, P.O. Box 1951, Los Angeles,
    Calif. 90028.
New Jersey Shakespeare Festival, Drew University, Madison, N.J.
    07940.
New York Shakespeare Festival, Public Theatre, 425 Lafayette
    St., New York, N.Y. 10003.

VI. Training Programs

For listings of the hundreds of undergraduate and graduate programs in the performing arts, write to the *Directory of American College Theater*, University and College Theater Association, 1029 Vermont Ave., NW, Washington, D.C. 20005. Below is a partial listing of graduate programs in drama, including those belonging to the League of Professional Theatre Training Programs.

Boston University School for the Arts, 855 Commonwealth Ave., Boston, Mass. 02214.

Brandeis University, South St., Waltham, Mass. 02154.

Carnegie-Mellon University, Dept. of Drama and Fine Arts, Pittsburgh, Penn. 15213.

Goodman School of Drama, Depaul University, 25 East Jackson Boulevard, Chicago, Ill. 60604.

The Juilliard School, Lincoln Center, New York, N.Y. 10023.

University of Minnesota, Duluth School of Fine Arts, Humanities 212, Duluth, Minn. 55812.

New York University, Washington Square, New York, N.Y. 10003.

North Carolina School of the Arts, P.O. Box 12189, Winston-Salem, N.C. 27107.

S.M.U. Meadows School of the Arts, Dallas, Texas 75275.

Temple University, Broad and Montgomery Sts., Philadelphia, Penn. 19122.

University of Washington, School of Drama BH-20, Seattle, Wash. 98195.

Yale University School of Drama, 1903-A Yale Station, New Haven, Conn. 06520.

VII. Service Organizations

This is a selective listing of those associations relating to or offering services to the individuals and institutions that make up the nonprofit professional theatre. For further information, write to the Theatre Communications Group, Inc., as listed below.

American Arts Alliance, 424 C St., NE, Washington, D.C. 20002. A coalition of more than 400 nonprofit professional performing and exhibiting institutions, the Alliance works at the federal level to affect legislation and to cultivate relationships with those who make federal arts policy.

American Council for the Arts, 570 7th Ave., New York, N.Y. 10018. Addressing management and policy needs of all the arts, A.C.A. provides books, informative packets, technical assistance, and training seminars.

American Theatre Association, Inc., 1029 Vermont Ave., NW, Washington, D.C. 20005. An organization primarily for individuals, community theatres, and educational institutions, A.T.A. sponsors the American College Theatre Festival, the Festival of American Community Theatre, conventions, publications, awards, and placement services.

Association of Hispanic Arts, 200 East 87th St., New York, N.Y. 10028. A.H.A. disseminates information on current Hispanic arts productions, with a bimonthly newsletter that includes an events calendar.

Black Theatre Alliance, 410 West 42nd St., New York, N.Y. 10036. B.T.A. provides a central clearinghouse for communications and information for black theatre and dance companies, and maintains a resume pool of artists and technicians, along with a technical training program.

Business Committee for the Arts, 1501 Broadway, New York, N.Y. 10036. B.C.A. encourages business and industry to support and become involved in the arts. Services and publications are free.

Center for Arts Information, 625 Broadway, New York, N.Y. 10012. The Center is a clearinghouse for information on the nonprofit arts.

Drama Book Shop, 150 West 52nd St., New York, N.Y. 10019. This bookstore devoted to the performing arts also publishes the quarterly *Annotated Bibliography of New Publications in the Performing Arts*, sold individually or by subscription. See Bibliography.

The Foundation Center, 888 7th Ave., New York, N.Y. 10016. Books, profiles, reports, and microfilm data on national and local private foundations illuminate the grantmaking process.

Foundation for the Extension and Development of the American Professional Theatre, 165 West 46th St., Suite 310, New York, N.Y. 10036. FEDAPT offers technical assistance in developing administrative and management capabilities in emerging and existing theatre and dance companies.

The Grantsmanship Center, 1031 South Grand Ave., Los Angeles, Calif. 90015. The Center provides nationwide training in program planning, resource development, and proposal preparation.

League of Professional Theatre Training Programs, 1860 Broadway, New York, N.Y. 10023. This alliance aims to improve training standards through resource and information sharing.

League of Resident Theatres, c/o The Guthrie Theatre, 725 Vineland Place, Minneapolis, Minn. 55403. A national association of nonprofit professional theatres operating under Equity LORT contracts, the League is active in labor relations, and concerns itself with the artistic and management needs of its members.

National Endowment for the Arts, 2401 E St., NW, Washington, D.C. and State Arts Councils, c/o the Office of the Attorney General in each state. These organizations are responsible for federal and local government endowments for arts and arts-related projects.

O'Neill Theatre Center, 1860 Broadway, New York, N.Y. 10023, and 305 Great Neck Road, Waterford, Conn. 06385. The O'Neill Center sponsors dozens of conferences, institutions, theatres, and publications, as well as new media production programs.

Opportunity Resources for the Arts, Inc., 1501 Broadway, New York, N.Y. 10036. OR is a nonprofit national placement service specializing in recruitment and referral of management personnel for arts organizations.

TAG Foundation, Ltd., 130 West 56th St., Room 905, New York, N.Y. 10019. TAG provides theatre and dance companies with information and assistance in production management, design referrals, and theatre specifications.

Theatre Development Fund, 1501 Broadway, Suite 2110, New York, N.Y. 10036. T.D.F. provides financial assistance and underwrites ticket voucher systems and reduced-rate ticket centers, and operates a costume collection for nonprofit performing arts organizations around the country.

Theatre Communications Group, Inc., 355 Lexington Ave., New York, N.Y. 10017. T.C.G. provides a variety of artistic, administrative, and informational programs to theatres and individual artists, administrators, and technicians, and acts as a forum for the profession and a resource for the media, funding agencies, and the public. T.C.G. publishes the annual *Theatre Profiles*, which features statistical, descriptive, historical, pictorial, and production information on nearly 170 companies, and is available for $12.95.

University/Resident Theatre Association, Inc., 1540 Broadway, Suite 704, New York, N.Y. 10036. URTA promotes a closer relationship between professional and university theatre.

Volunteer Lawyers for the Arts, 36 West 44th St., Suite 1110, New York, N.Y. 10036. V.L.A. arranges free legal representation and provides legal information to individual artists with income below $7,500 and nonprofit arts organizations with budgets under $100,000 that have arts-related legal problems.

UNIONS

The following is a list of the main unions related to the theatre.

Actors' Equity Association, 165 West 46th St., New York, N.Y. 10036.

American Federation of Television and Radio Actors, 1350 Avenue of the Americas, New York, N.Y. 10019.

American Guild of Musical Artists, 1841 Broadway, New York, N.Y. 10023.

International Alliance of Theatre and Stage Employees, 1515 Broadway, New York, N.Y. 10036.

Screen Actors' Guild, 1700 Broadway, New York, N.Y. 10023.

Index